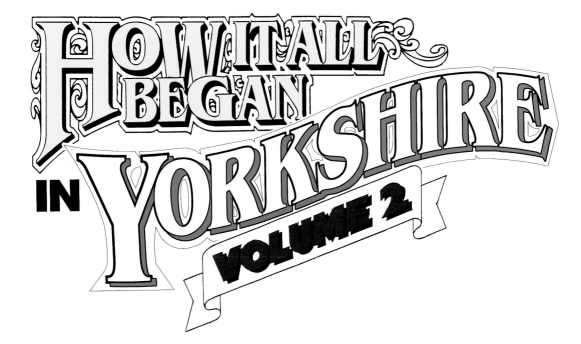

How It All Began in Yorkshire

Volume 2

First published in Great Britain 2000 by
Dalesman Publishing Company Limited
Stable Courtyard, Broughton Hall
Skipton, North Yorkshire BD23 3AE

Text © Maurice Baren

A British Library Cataloguing in Publication record
is available for this book

ISBN 1 85568 183-8
Colour Origination by Compass Reprographics
Printed by Midas Printing (HK) Limited

FOREWORD

Some of my earliest cricketing memories are of Maurice Leyland, who helped me so much at the Yorkshire nets – he was a real gentleman and one of Yorkshire and England's great all-rounders. The author's mother was a cousin of Maurice Leyland and Maurice takes his name from the kindly man. Like myself Maurice is also grateful for his Methodist heritage, something I still cherish today.

I was born in Barnsley and therefore can recall the nearby Redfearn glassworks and Samuel Fox – the makers of umbrella frames. Perhaps as a child, a fonder South Yorkshire product was Bassett's Liquorice Allsorts, made up the road in Sheffield.

Like Maurice's earlier book on Yorkshire firms, *How It All Began in Yorkshire*, this book also tells the fascinating stories behind names I have known all my life. It is difficult to believe that Comet, the well-known electrical store, should have started by renting out accumulators to power those old wireless sets, or how Marks & Spencer started in Leeds only three or four miles from those cricket nets at Headingley that I went to on the tram all those years ago.

How life has changed – from the corner grocer's shop I knew in Barnsley to the large supermarkets such as Morrisons which we all go to today. And how good it was to read of the early life of Alf Wight, better known to most of us as James Herriot. This book is certainly full of nostalgia and surprises – I'm sure it will revive memories for all who read it. Good luck, Maurice.

DICKIE BIRD

AUTHOR'S NOTE

I dedicate this book to a true Yorkshireman – Dr Fred Kidd MA, FRSA, FTI
Over the last decade he has been a real encouragement to me in my writing.
He has kept me regularly occupied with clippings and information on a wide range of subjects.
Fred's help has been much appreciated.

Each story in this book is the story of the coming together of a number of people, and I could not have completed this compilation without their help. It is always said to be dangerous to name names for fear of missing out someone – I certainly will not do it intentionally, and if I have forgotten you I do apologise, and will try and remedy it in future editions.

A number of people have loaned me books, or pointed me towards obscure works that have been a source of good information, and often not a few laughs, thank you. To large companies and small firms who have let me borrow from their valuable personal archives I am grateful for this co-operation and trust. However, I would like to thank the following who have been particularly helpful: Charles Barker, Mrs Johnson, Marie Jackson, Michael Hollingbery, Allen Rowley, Nigel Veal, Mrs Lobb, Tracey Cawton, Rachel Roberts, Martin Tilstone, Don Hutton, Barbara Gent, Isobel Hunter, Jenny Bryan, Raymond Needler, Jim Wight, L W McCormick, Joe Walton, Dr Fred Kidd and Stewart Brown as well as Ackworth School, Hutton Press, Hull University Archives, Pan Macmillan, Marketing by Design and The Scottish Daily Record (for its kind permission to use the photograph on page 113 and the front cover). Tom Hewitt, as ever, has created another great jacket and Barbara Allen has been responsible for the design of the book. The staff of the Dalesman Publishing Company are a constant source of support, particularly Robert Flanagan and Rachel Allen. Finally, my continued thanks go to my wife Judith for her help with research, and in so many other ways.

CONTENTS

INTRODUCTION

Two years ago I brought together my first selection of stories of Yorkshire businesses, *How It All Began in Yorkshire*, which was so well received that the Dalesman Publishing Company has suggested we look at another range of companies. As before, the list includes well known companies which started in the county and are now household names throughout the British Isles, whereas others are still only known in the area where they were created, but none-the-less have an interesting story, which is a valuable part of our social history.

William Greensmith, a gentleman's outfitters in Harrogate, was an influential tradesman, and member of the Harrogate Improvement Commissioners, when that now popular shopping town's fashionable streets were first being laid down. He was also a prominent Methodist, but across at Ackworth a group of Quakers sought to find ways to alleviate suffering among members of their own beliefs who might fall on hard times – the result was the formation of the Friends' Provident. Similarly it was the difficulties one man had in securing a mortgage which led to the formation of the Ecology Building Society, which was only created in 1981.

I am sure that each town, and indeed many villages, have a story to tell of industrial or commercial development. Across in Whitby on our beautiful coastline Fortune's kippers have been favourites among locals and visitors for many a year, whilst further south, in Hull, Comet, the electrial suppliers began by hiring out accumulators – can you remember 'accumulators'? As we move east we come to the Sheffield area where sheep shears have been supplied to distant lands for over 150 years, and where for a similar time people have been drawing wire and making the frames for umbrellas. Journeying north we come to Leeds where one of the country's best known stores, Marks & Spencer, was founded and where Wallace Arnold, one of the country's best known coach operators is based. Completing our circular tour in the northern most part of Yorkshire in Northallerton, we have the story of Barkers, yet another of the county's success stories.

However, in between are about another thirty fascinating tales of initiative, endeavour, hard work and dedication – I hope you enjoy reading about people of grit, people who have been proud of the White Rose, proud to be Yorkshire folk.

Ackrill media group

The company's Cardale Park premises and (inset)
J W Ackrill, son of the founder

Harrogate has had its own 'newspaper' since 1820 – *The Weekly List of the Company at Harrogate*, which was published by William Langdale of High Harrogate and was simply a list of visitors to the town.

However, in 1821 Pickersgill Pallister, a Cleveland man, arrived in town with half-a-crown in his pocket and a desire to make his fortune. At first he opened a school in Cornwall Road, but after ten years gave that up to begin a career in printing and stationery. On 8 September 1834 he launched his *List of Visitors* – which recorded people staying at hotels and guest houses in the town. It was of little interest to local people, but visitors were encouraged to call in at the office and give their details – no doubt they enjoyed seeing their name in print.

Two years later, on 26 September 1836, he launched *The Harrogate Advertiser and Weekly List of Visitors* from near the Well in Low Harrogate,

probably close to where Royal Parade now stands. However, it only ran for a few weeks, ceasing publication at the end of October (the end of the season), not to recommence until the following June. In 1837 publication day was switched to Saturdays, and to emphasise that the paper was intended for visitors, Pickersgill Pallister left one page blank so that they could write a letter on it, and then post the whole paper at letter rate! Advertisements carried in those early newspapers included ones for the provision of education at 'Grove House', High Harrogate, where Mr Stubbs offered young gentlemen 'Education in the English, Latin and Greek Languages; Writing, Accounts, Mathematics, Bookkeeping, &c. &c.'; Smeeton & Lawson, Silk Mercers, Lace-men, Hosiers & Glovers; a note that bottled

Harrogate Mineral Water can be sent to all parts of the Kingdom *direct from the Well*, by S Blackburn, Library, Low Harrogate; and among others a large advertisement drawing attention to the activities of P Palliser at the Advertiser Office.

A year later, on the death of George IV, the paper's pages carried a black boundary, and P Bown of the Free Museum in High Harrogate declared that he had Jet Ornaments of every description for sale, at the usual prices, 'suitable for the present GENERAL MOURNING'.

The issue of 14 September 1837 reported that the Harrogate Bath Hospital had reopened with about 20 patients being admitted. On the same day an election for an extra surgeon took place, and a Mr Abrose Cookson of High Harrogate was appointed. That issue also contained information on the Annual Dress Ball which had been held at the Dragon Hotel, 'and was, as usual, attended by the beauty and fashion of Harrogate and the neighbourhood. Many of the families came from a distance of 14 and 15 miles. We never remember having seen on any similar occasion, so great an assemblage of elegantly dressed Ladies. Nearly 300 fashionables were present.'

As the town developed rapidly in the 1840s a group of businessmen decided to launch a rival newspaper, the *Harrogate Herald*. It was first published on 6 May 1847, and was owned by William Dawson who was also a printer and stationer. The paper was printed in Leeds and brought to Harrogate on a mule and cart. The editor of the *Harrogate Herald* was Robert Ackrill, a 30 year old former printer, who came to Leeds from Worcester – the paper took the Liberal

political viewpoint, whilst the *Harrogate Advertiser* adopted a Conservative stance.

Among the advertisements, which filled its front page, was one announcing that William Greensmith had just opened his Hosiery and Lace Establishment in High Harrogate, whilst others include George Renton, Sherriff's Officer, Auctioneer and Bailiff; The Cocoa Tree Tea Establishment in Leeds; the Atlas Assurance Company Fire Department at 92 Cheapside in London; and the Harlow Carr Hotel and Sulphureous Alkaline Springs and Baths, at Harlow Carr, near Harrogate. W Dawson, the paper's proprietor, announced on page 2 that at his Victoria News Room subscribers could see copies of daily and weekly papers and periodicals, which included the following daily papers: *The London Times, Morning Herald, Morning Post, Evening Sun, Standard* and the *Daily News*; Weeklies such as: *Leeds Intelligencer, Manchester Guardian, Dublin Evening Mail, Illustrated London News* and *Punch*; and periodicals including: *Blackwood's Edinburgh Magazine, Bentley's Miscellany*, and *United Services Journal*.

On 13 May 1847 it told its readers that it claimed to 'speak with the frankness, if not of an old friend, yet of one whose heart is set upon making Harrogate not only the most delightful but also the most frequented of Britain's inland Watering Places'. It went on to recall that it was in 1770 that an Act of Parliament was passed enacting that the 'Strays' (or 'Parks' according to our modern nomenclature) to the extent of two hundred acres, 'should remain unenclosed for the comfort and accommodation of the gentry visiting here for the benefit of our air and waters'. However, having seen the parks drained in recent years and seats placed at convenient places along pathways it stressed the need to adorn the open spaces with rows or clumps of trees and larger shrubs and such like. The proprietors of the paper also called for an end to the rivalry between High and Low Harrogate, they having decided to not acknowledge such divisions.

At the 1841 census Harrogate had a population of about 500; by 1847 it had grown substantially.

As early as August 1847 antagonism had grown between the two papers, after the *Harrogate Advertiser* had cast dirt upon its opponent. The *Harrogate Herald*, in response, claimed that they would not have had to come into being had it not been for 'last year's contemptible visitors' list' which the *Harrogate Advertiser* produced, and its reluctance to accede to reasonable requests.

In the issue of the *Harrogate Herald* of 28 October 1847 we are told that the paper was established 'by the purely public-spirited efforts of its Proprietors, whose sole object was that of securing to Harrogate a newspaper independent of sect or party – a newspaper which should contain nothing calculated to offend the most fastidious – a newspaper devoted to the welfare and progressive improvement of this delightful watering-place'.

Once again, at the end of the season, it was going to close down until the following summer, but it went on to promise its readers that on its reappearance it would be in future printed in the town 'upon new and elegant type . . . which will double the present amount of news'. It was also going to devote its attention to the happenings in the nearby towns of Ripon, Knaresbro', and Wetherby, together with Ripley and Harewood. From the next year it would also become a permanent newspaper, rather than a seasonal one.

However, in 1858 the *Harrogate Advertiser* was bought by Thomas Hollins and became filled with local, national and international news, and was published weekly throughout the year. It was now very much a paper for the residents, although the List of Visitors was still published.

During the mid 19th century the *Harrogate Advertiser* gave details of 'Post Office Regulations', naming Mr P Palliser as Postmaster at offices opposite Westmoreland Street in High Harrogate with the Receiving House being at Blackburn's Library near the Crown Hotel in Low Harrogate.

Letters arrived, from such places as: London, Liverpool, Leeds, Bradford, the South and West of England and from Ireland at quarter past six in the evening; and from Scotland, the North and East Ridings, Northumberland, Cumberland, Westmorland, County Durham, Thirsk, Knaresboro, York, and Hull at eight in the morning. Departures to the first group were at half past nine in the evening and five in the morning, whilst post for the latter destinations left at half past one at night.

Letters and newspapers were delivered to hotels and houses in High and Low Harrogate, both morning and evening, or could be had at the office window half an hour after their arrival. The letter box closed at half past nine 'precisely', although letters for London and the South and West of England, and for Ireland, would be received up to twenty minutes before ten, on payment of one penny, and as late as ten o'clock on payment of six pence.

In 1870 Pickersgill Pallister who had launched the *Harrogate Advertiser*, retired from his subsequent work, that of Postmaster at Harrogate, an appointment made by the Postmaster General. The Board of the Improvement Commissioners wrote expressing appreciation of his 33 years service.

During the 1870s Robert Ackrill bought the *Harrogate Advertiser* from Thomas Hollins and founded Ackrill Newspapers. In 1878 Ellen, Robert Ackrill's daughter, married William Hammond Breare, who was then editing the *Harrogate Herald* for Robert Ackrill – the Breare dynasty was to last until 1983, when Robert Roddick Ackrill Breare sold the company to United Newspapers. William Breare edited the *Harrogate Herald* for over 50 years, and Jack W Ackrill, Robert's son, was proprietor and editor of the *Harrogate Advertiser* until his death in 1915.

However, in 1884 Robert Ackrill had the honour of being the town's Charter Mayor, and was handed by Mr Bateson, solicitor to the Improvement Commissioners, the long sought charter which made the town a Borough, and which brought to an end the role of the Improvement Commissioners in favour of the newly formed Corporation.

J W Ackrill was also involved in civic affairs and was a founder member of the Conservative Club and a member of the Literary Club. He also played rugby for the town and was elected an honorary life member of the Harrogate Cricket

Club. At his funeral the council was represented by the Mayor and Town Clerk. The Town Clerk later wrote: 'This Council place on record its high appreciation of the long and invaluable services rendered to the town by the late Mr J W Ackrill, who for many years past has assisted and supported all movements for the good of the inhabitants and the prosperity of the borough.'

Over the years the Ackrill Group has increased its coverage with such papers as the *Nidderdale Herald*, *Northallerton Thirsk and Bedale Times*, *Knaresborough Post* and *The Ripon Gazette*. However, the Group's readership is worldwide, for its papers go to Tykes in exile throughout the world.

Since the Second World War the Ackrill Group has purchased the *Pudsey Times* and the *Wetherby News*. During these later years the papers have reported on such controversies as the development of Harrogate's Conference Centre and the redevelopment of the Market area, as well as bringing news on the lives of ordinary people, business and commerce.

For many years Ackrill newspapers were located at the bottom of Montpellier Parade but Regional Independent Media, which now owns the Group, is based in new buildings at Harlow Hill on the outskirts of Harrogate. There, the latest technology is used to produce a portfolio of newspapers serving the local communities. The *Harrogate Advertiser* and the *Harrogate Herald* have developed far beyond what their founders might have visualised over 150 years ago.

R. ACKRILL,

PRINTER, LITHOGRAPHER, BOOKBINDER, AND + + + + DIE STAMPER. + + + + + +

ACCOUNT BOOK MANUFACTURER,

Herald Printing Works,

Montpellier Street and Gardens, Low Harrogate.

Printing, Bookbinding, and Lithography of every description done on the premises.

Ledgers, Day Books, Cash Books, Journals, Ruled and Bound to any pattern.

Letter Books made to any shape or style.

Machine Ruling of every description executed on the shortest notice.

Music Binding in Limp, Roan, or Cloth, a Speciality.

Andrassy
Marquees Ltd.

Burghley horse trials, 1999

In the 19th century certain members of the Andrassy family were Hungarian aristocrats, including Count Julius – a handsome patriot who became Prime Minister of Hungary. A poorer Andrassy family who lived in southern Germany were thought to be linked to the Hungarian line. The eldest of their six sons, Charles, decided to seek his fortune in England and became a pork butcher in Keighley. Later he sent for his two brothers and sister to join him.

George Frederick Andrassy was only 15 when he also became a pork butcher – in Leigh Street, Wakefield in 1877. Eventually he took on catering, hiring marquees to support the initiative. The marquee company was established in 1887 in Thornes Lane, Wakefield.

He had decided to buy a tent, take it to

Catalogue shot from the forties showing camp equipment for the military, Boys Brigade and Girl Guides

pieces and use it as a pattern to make more. It must have been a slow and laborious task – hand sewing the canvas to make a marquee – and he would sit long into the night stitching whilst singing hymns. It would be equally arduous loading all the poles and canvas onto a horse and cart, yet even with such a limited means of transportation he was still able to offer a service selling and hiring out the equipment over a 10 mile radius around Wakefield. In those early days the functions he worked at would be mainly shooting parties, garden parties and agricultural shows. He slowly became a successful businessman.

During the 1914-1918 war he did a great deal of work for the War Ministry and eventually became a naturalised British subject. After the war, when his three sons returned home (he had married a girl from his home town in Germany), he started the Wakefield Transport Company to complement the seasonal element of the

A traditional wedding, 1999

Pictures from a 1960 catalogue: Powder room with Racasan toilets, dressing tables and running hot and cold water – "if required" and a marquee with places for 1,600 provided for the Royal opening of a Welsh steelworks

marquee company's work. The wagons were Maudsleys with solid tyres and oil lamps, and the company was the first in Wakefield to have covered cabs to protect the drivers from the elements.

After his death in 1930 the family business was taken over by his sons, Frederic, Adolphus and Herbert. By now the workload was expanding rapidly to provide tentage for weddings, scout camps, hospital camps, various organisations,

*Nightclub themed marquee
for a summer ball*

and, of course, for the ever-growing number of agricultural shows.

Unfortunately the Second World War brought a stop to many of these events and business opportunities were severely limited. After the war Frederic Andrassy was later joined by his sons George and Gerald, Adolphus and Herbert having retired.

George worked tirelessly and with great enthusiasm and once again the business showed rapid growth. In 1973 Frederic died and in 1974 Gerald retired leaving George to run the firm. He moved the business to Lofthouse, Wakefield. Later Charles, George's son, entered the business and today it is run by Jacquie Andrassy.

In 1997 Andrassy Marquees Ltd moved to new state-of-the-art premises in South Yorkshire from where the firm provides tentage for such prestigious events as the horse trials at Burghley, Gatcombe Park and Bramham, the Embassy World Snooker Event, as well as providing venues for weddings, bar mitzvahs, themed balls, corporate events and parties for people of all ages.

Now tentage and marquees can create a temporary extension to a home, a colour co-ordinated ballroom, or be totally themed to link to the event being planned. Excellent floor surfaces, lighting and heating enables the modern marquee with its drapes and quality furniture to be functional both in summer and winter.

No doubt George Frederick Andrassy would be amazed at how the industry has developed and the high standards that have been attained today.

William Armitage was born at Skelmanthorpe, near Huddersfield, in 1808. His early days were spent as a cloth miller at Cawthorne but after he married Ann Bell, the daughter of the landlord of the Golden Cross public house in Cawthorne, he opened a shop near to the Horse Wells and became a confectioner. Following several changes of premises, in 1842 he opened a shop in Huddersfield's Beast Market. That same year he started selling seeds, conducting his business from that shop for the next 14 years – this is the start of the Armitage Garden Centre business we know today.

However, he eventually disagreed with his landlord over politics, and so moved his business to 4 New Street, in the centre of the town, trading as a corn and seed

William Armitage

warehouse. The catalogue for the 'Huddersfield Seed Warehouse' lists 834 items of flower seed, and has a section containing 23 selections of German flower seeds, these being a speciality of Armitage's at that time.

In the 1864 catalogue of vegetables and agricultural seeds he lists 37 varieties of peas, 17 varieties of French beans, 19 varieties of celery, and 20 varieties of onion. On the back cover he also draws his customers' attention to the fact that he supplies bedding plants to order, Brown & Polson's patent cornflour, that he is an importer of Russian flour and other foreign produce, sells Armitage's Superior Cut Groats which are very good for invalids, oil cake and guano,

Russian mats, Cuba bass and cocoa nut refuse – he was certainly ahead of his time on the last one! At one time the firm also had nurseries at Primrose Hill and Fenay Bridge on the outskirts of Huddersfield. From a booklet which he published in the 1880s, entitled 'WORTH READING! Notes on Vegetable Gardening, Mushroom Growing, Lawns, Croquet & Cricket Grounds', we discover some of the practices of

the day for eliminating pests, diseases and other problems. For fumigating, a recommendation is to heat torn tobacco paper with a candle, whilst for destroying weeds on walks it was recommended to 'Dissolve 1lb of powdered arsenic in 3 gallons of cold water and boil it, stirring it well on the fire; then add 7 gallons of water holding in solution 2lbs of soda, boil and stir again, applying it when hot to the walks.' It also reprints a letter from the *Gardeners' Chronicle* which gives a recipe to be used as a spray or dip to kill greenfly – 'Half a pound of soft soap dissolved (but not boiled) in soft water, 2ozs of strong tobacco (common shag) boiled for an hour with 1oz of bitter aloes; mix with 3 gallons of warm soft water.' Similarly, what would seem to us dangerous today, is where the suggestion that sulphuric acid is used to kill plantains, dandelions and thistles in lawns – 'We do not dilute the acid at all for this purpose' – it was applied to the centre of the plant by using a

xxviii. WM. ARMITAGE & SON, SEED MERCHANTS,

SUNDRY GARDEN REQUISITES.

FIR TREE OIL INSECTICIDE,
1/3, 2/1, 3/9, 6/6 per Bottle.

GISHURST'S COMPOUND
1/- per Box

ARCHANGEL MATS.

COCOA FIBRE REFUSE,
4 Bushels, 2/6.

Fern Soil, 2/6 per Bushel.

Potting Soil, 1/6 per Bushel.

Standen's Manure, Gardeners' & Amateurs' Friend.
1/- per Tin.

Tobacco Paper, dry and extra strong.
1/- per pound.

TOBACCO POWDER.
1/- per Tin.

FLORIST GUM, 1/- PER BOTTLE.

foot-long stick about the thickness of a pencil. Needless to say these ideas should NOT be tried today.

William and Ann had four children – Tamar, Emma, Bell (Ann's maiden name), and William. When Bell joined him in the business it became William Armitage & Son. William Armitage was decidely Liberal in his political views. For 14 years he was treasurer of the Huddersfield Permanent Benefit Building Society, and for some years was connected with the Huddersfield Secular Society. Before his death he expressed a wish that he might die on the anniversary of his birth – he died on his 68th birthday, 8th May 1876! Recognising William's views the Unitarian minister divided the service into two parts, one for those who held views similar to the deceased, the other for his Christian friends.

Bell and his wife Elizabeth had five children – Edward, Bell, Tom, Charles and Fanny, and Bell and Tom joined the business. Tom married Harriett Quinton, and as Bell passed down two generations, in a similar way the name Quinton

was given to Bell's elder son. The firm's nurseries were closed down after the First World War and the agricultural supplies business was discontinued after the Second World War.

In 1963 the firm moved to larger premises at 1 Lord Street, and there started selling garden furniture and garden machinery, the latter being developed by Quinton Armitage, Bell's son. Initially machinery repairs were carried out in the basement of the premises but later the firm took over a garage in the Beast Market. Following further growth of the garden machinery trade, that aspect of the business moved to new premises in Old Leeds Road where there was a showroom and workshop under the same roof.

When Pennine Garden Centre came on the market in 1985 this was added to the business, and in 1991 a rather run-down nursery at Birkencliffe was acquired and converted into a second garden centre, replacing the town centre locations. The present partners are Quinton and Alistair Armitage, ably and enthusiastically assisted by several other members of the family.

The Barker family can truly claim to be Northallerton born and bred, for its members have lived there since 1631. For over 200 years, every one of them was a farmer until young William, who was born in 1868, decided to do something different.

William Barker and family

William Barker started as an apprentice at John Oxendale's draper's shop in Northallerton's High Street in 1882, agreeing to serve a six year term. He was bound by his indenture to keep his master's secrets, gladly do his lawful commands, not contract matrimony within the set term, not to play at dice or card tables, not smoke nor haunt taverns or playhouses, nor absence himself from his master's service unlawfully by day or night – 'But in all things as a faithful Apprentice he shall behave himself towards his said Master and all his during the said term'. Each Sunday he had to attend a place of worship twice, and his father had to promise to provide his son with sufficient clothes, washing, medicines, and other necessities during the six years.

Assistants outside Oxendale & Barkers around 90 years ago

However, John Oxendale did have to supply young William with sufficient meat, drink and lodgings for the term of the apprenticeship.

The business which had started in 1875 later became Oxendale & Barker and in 1912 they ran a half-page advertisement in Smithson's North-allerton Almanack, offering suits for sale. Up until the end of the First World War the store specialised in fabrics and millinery — goods included hessians, dress fabrics, shirtings, tweeds, cottons, linens, blanket wools, sheeting and even brush braids to protect the hems of ladies' skirts as they walked around the streets.

William may have been a person of small stature but he was an astute businessman and eventually bought out John Oxendale — the store then becoming William Barker's. Even after his retirement he came into the town on his bicycle and regularly came into the shop — the staff always left a duster handy, and even though they would have dusted the counter that morning, it was his ritual to ensure it had been done properly, and do it again!

William's son Leslie well remembered the store, when as a lad of eight, he used to go to the shop with his father's lunch. He recorded how the errand boy would take purchases out to the customer's horse drawn trap, and how on market day people would also arrive in gigs, carts, four-wheeled-wagons and by steam train. Horses would be

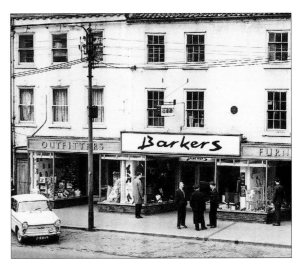

stabled at nearby hotels and then the many farmers' wives would go off and sell their eggs, butter or fruit before commencing their own shopping.

In 1921 Leslie joined his father and brothers, Wilfred and Lawrence, in the family firm. Leslie had a good memory for figures and used to buy stocks and shares for other members of the family. Still in the 1930s the brothers were joined by Mike Scales and Don Raper; Don, now a Board member, is on most days to be found

John Everson

Charles Barker (left) with John Raper (son of Don)

working in the store – his only break of employment was during service in the RAF in the Second World War! Over the 65 or so years he has been involved in Barkers, starting as an errand boy, he has seen many changes and great developments. Initially the shop was long and narrow, but one by one neighbouring shops were bought and added on. The furniture department started in the premises on the High Street now occupied by the Co-op. In the 1920s,

normal days were from 9am to 6pm, although on a Saturday it might be as late as 8.30pm before Don could fix the iron gate on the front of the premises. Before he could lock up he had to take lengths of suiting, which had been cut to size, to the railway station for them to be transported to Berwin the tailors in Leeds. Although staff had had a break at lunchtime there were no official tea breaks; however, some would sneak out to the shop next door with a hat box, and in it bring back a jam puff and some tea and be secretly refreshed in the boiler room!

Leslie started the footwear department and this was further developed by Don, who would accompany him on visits to Leicester to buy shoes from the manufacturers, and later by Maureen Carr who still manages the department, having come to Barkers straight from school in 1956. John Rawson, a chairman of one of the shoe companies, was blind and yet he would sell them shoes by touch as he could readily recognise one style and size from another, knowing each one by a number. Barkers would often buy broken ranges and of course, belonging to a farming community, boots which were guaranteed waterproof were an important part of their trade.

By 1934 the firm had become William Barker & Sons, and had a branch at 48 Market Place, Thirsk as well as the shop in Northallerton High Street (which incidentally had an easily remembered telephone number, Northallerton 123!).

At this time Barkers was in business as a Furnishers, Milliners, Tailors and Hosiers. During the war years it supplied yard upon yard of black dyed cotton cloth to be used as blackout; many officers also came to them to be fitted and supplied with their uniforms.

On an October morning in 1946 William Barker visited some stock in a field, then cycled up the town to the store before going to a horse show and sale at the Applegarth Mart in Northallerton; however, while he was there he suddenly collapsed and died – he was 78 years old. In addition to his business interests he had been a fine horseman, a member of the Urban District Council for 17 years, and a deacon at Zion Congregational Church.

About this time Barkers became a limited company and started to expand by acquiring

Barkers 125th anniversary photograph

Marcus Grover

adjoining properties, these being developed to increase the range of goods on offer. New lines included china and glass, soaps and perfumes, cookware, and a restaurant. Now they could really call themselves a department store.

In 1970 Leslie's son Charles joined the management team, having gained experience in the family store as well as in one of the country's leading businesses. Today he is managing director.

During the early 1980s Barkers purchased land adjoining the main store, even though there was a right of way through it. However, it developed an arcade which encompassed the right of way and in 1985 Barkers Arcade opened for trade. It contains twelve tenanted shops which vary in range from a goldsmith to shops selling books and men and women's clothing.

The furniture department moved to a site in Yafforth Road in 1994 which has made way for further expansion within the main store, this having resulted in several awards, including in 1998 'Lingerie Department of the Year' from the trade magazine *Drapers Record*. Whilst many department stores have found the going hard over the last decade, Barkers continues to go from strength to strength.

One important visitor returns to the store each year, arriving in a stagecoach, driven by George Bowman, a champion four-in-hand driver – Santa Claus is always greeted by hundreds of people who gather in the High Street. It is the start of a hectic selling period, but one where the store and community retain their close links.

TREBOR BASSETT

When the Cluniac monks came from France and established a monastery in Pontefract in the 11th century, they brought with them liquorice plants, which grew well in the deep soils around the town. The remains of a medieval pharmacy have been found nearby, and it is likely

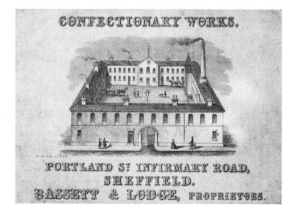

that liquorice was extracted from the roots of the plants, for use in the preparation of medicines.

After the dissolution of the monasteries local farmers continued to grow liquorice and a cottage industry grew up making liquorice lozenges which were taken to ease stomach disorders.

About 1769 a Pontefract chemist, George Dunhill, produced the first 'Pomfret Cake', Pomfret being the old name for Pontefract. These early sweetmeats were also known as Yorkshire Pennies, because of their origin and shape. Local confectioners

made the liquorice sweets into other shapes such as the Catherine wheels, bootlaces, pipes, etc, we know today.

However, the story of liquorice was not to be confined to Pontefract for over in Sheffield a major confectionery company was created in the 1840s. Its founder was

George Bassett

George Bassett, who was born in Ashover, near Chesterfield in 1818, the third of John Bassett's eight children. He had been a woolcomber but because of the depression had turned to farming. Whilst poor in worldly terms, George's parents were devoted Christians and bequeathed these principles to their children. The children's education was gained at the village school, at a cost of 3d to 4d each per week, supplemented by the free education they received at the Methodist Sunday School. Sadly George's father died while he was only twelve years old, but a few years before his death he had written down the following advice to his children:

'My dear children, I think it probable that I may be taken from you while you are young; and as your welfare lies near my heart, I feel desirous of leaving you some advice, which I entreat you to observe. A little consideration will convince you that I have no end in view but your good. I

have lived long enough to know something of human life (being now fifty years of age) and to form a judgement of what is best to be pursued, and what ought to be avoided in the journey of life.

The first, and most important duty of life,

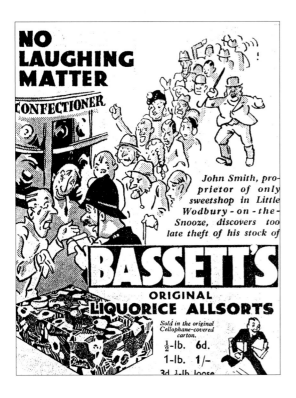

and to which every other thing should be subservient, is the care of your immortal souls; for if you lose your souls you lose your all . . . But beware of taking a round of duties for religion; . . . A change must take place in your hearts; your affections must be set on things above, and not on things below.

The second is to be careful of your health. To this end, it is good to avoid all intemperance, to avoid running into danger, and to use exercise in the open air.

The third thing I advise you to, is to be prudent and careful in the management of the little property I leave you. With care, it may

help to put you in a way to live comfortably; but if you are wild and extravagant, it will soon be spent, and you will be forced to labour hard for a scanty subsistence . . .

Be obedient to your Mother. Be kind to one another. Be strictly honest. Never tell a lie. Make it a rule to attend some place of worship regularly. Always keep in your minds that God sees you.'

When George was fourteen he was apprenticed for seven years to a confectioner and fruiterer, William Haslam of Chesterfield. He stayed with Mr Haslam a further three years before buying a small retail confectionery and wine business at 30 Broad Street in the Park district of Sheffield. In the 1845 Directory of Traders George Bassett is shown as the new proprietor and is described as a Wholesale Confectioner, Lozenge Maker and British Wine Dealer. It was between 1841 and 1845 that Bassett's business began, most probably 1842, and within a few years he had three other shops.

George married his first wife Sarah Hodgson in 1842 and they had eight children: six girls and two boys who both died in infancy. After Sarah's death in 1862 he later married again and had two further sons.

In 1851 he took as an apprentice a lad of twelve, Samuel Meggitt Johnson. Samuel's mother had died

and his father, who had a retail furniture business, had married again, and therefore Samuel went to live with the Bassett family.

At the end of his apprenticeship Samuel went back to work for his father. George Bassett, however, acquired larger premises in Portland Street, and later took a local grocer, William Lodge, into partnership. This arrangement did not work out, and in 1860 George persuaded Samuel to return, on the understanding that he would soon become a partner. In 1863 Samuel reminded George of that promise and he not only became a partner, but later sole proprietor, staying with the business a further 62 years.

By 1862 George Bassett was employing nearly 150 people making lozenges, liquorice comfits, pate de ju-jubes, acid drops, candied peel, marmalade and Pontefract cakes. The firm's products sold all over the country and were also exported to various parts of the world. A contemporary writer described the works as 'the largest and most complete of their kind in this or any other country.'

He also took a great interest in local politics and became Mayor of Sheffield in 1876. During his year of office, General Ulysses S Grant, famous soldier of the American Civil War and President of the United States, who was completing his term of Presidency, visited Sheffield and stayed at George Bassett's home in Endcliffe Crescent. In 1876 the premises at Portland Street were extended by the addition of another factory – to celebrate its completion he invited his entire staff to have tea with him in the Mayor's parlour. Over 200 attended and he was presented with an illuminated address to celebrate his election to the Mayoralty of Sheffield.

In 1878 he had a paralytic stroke and after further attacks gave up all his public and business interests. He died in 1886, aged 68.

Samuel Meggitt Johnson had married George Bassett's eldest daughter in 1868, but she died in childbirth 18 months later. Samuel now took control of the business, founding the Don Confectionery Company for George's sons, but with himself as senior partner. Following a serious fire at Bassett's factory in 1892 (which caused Samuel to have a nervous breakdown as he was inadequately

insured) and a family dispute, he became sole proprietor of Bassett's but severed all links with the Don Confectionery Company, although in 1933 George's last remaining son, John, sold out to Bassett's.

In the mid 1870s Samuel married again and they had three sons, who were away at boarding school at the time of the fire. He could no longer afford to keep them at school, so they entered the business while their father went to Italy to recover. The younger ones, William and Percy, were only 15 and 13. It was they who gradually took over the management of the company.

For many years prior to 1899 Bassett's produced a range of liquorice cream lines, which together with solid liquorice units and military buttons were sold separately. It had at that time four full-time travellers, one of these being Charlie Thompson (who died in harness in 1946, having served the firm for 61 years). One day he was visiting a customer called Walker, in Leicester, and had placed his sample tray on a chair while he talked to his customer. A lady assistant unfortunately knocked it to the floor and the various sweets fell out. Charlie moved them together with his foot, but suddenly Mr Walker exclaimed, 'I rather like the look of that assortment. Ask your firm if they will supply me with all sorts mixed together.' – Liquorice Allsorts had been born!

In 1900 a factory was built at Owlerton where candied peel, gums, pastilles and other goods were made; this traded under the name of S M Johnson & Sons, whilst Liquorice Allsorts, lozenges, panned goods and plain liquorice lines were made at Bassett's Portland Street factory. During the First World War the factory at Owlerton made jam, when sugar restrictions reduced the amount of confectionery they were permitted to make.

Bassett's went 'public' in 1926, following the death of Samuel Johnson in 1925, and decided to look for a trademark. The task was given to the Greenlys Advertising Agency. The 'Michelin Man' had been advertising the Michelin tyre products successfully, and Mr Bull, Greenlys managing director, suggested that Bassett's should use something similar. 'Bertie Bassett', a character created from pieces of liquorice confectionery, was the answer. Over the years he has changed, acquiring a face and a walking stick, but Bertie is still very popular and identified as Bassett's!

In 1966 Bassett's acquired Barratt, a firm famous for its sherbet fountains. In the 1980s the Crediton, Devon-based firm Ernest Jackson & Co Ltd, who make Victory V Lozenges and Zubes, and also Anglo Bellamy and Beech-Nut Sweets, joined the group. Today Trebor Bassett is part of the large Cadbury Schweppes group.

Today many young people grow up and enter the world of work only to find within a few years that the world around them has moved on and they also may have to refocus their future. Perhaps thirty or forty years ago many more people were inclined to stay within their chosen career for the whole of their working lives – forty, fifty years or more! Not so Lawrence Batley.

Lawrence Batley, the son of an engineer, was born in Bland Street, Lockwood in 1911. He went to Birkby Council School before moving on to Hillhouse Central School, which he left at the age of 14. During his school days he enjoyed the arts side, but was bad at subjects such as physics, chemistry and maths – something which would be vitally important to him later in life. However, he thoroughly enjoyed sport, particularly rugby league, and went on to captain the Yorkshire boys' side, playing on every major league ground in Yorkshire.

On leaving school he got a job in the solicitors office of Mills & Best, before going to work at the YMCA, and then becoming an insurance salesman.

In 1939 he joined the RAF, hoping to become a pilot, but his balance was not sufficiently good to allow him to become aircrew, and when the opportunity came he was only too pleased to be demobbed.

Returning to civilian life in 1945 he became a pharmaceutical salesman, later becoming area manager for the north of England. By now Lawrence was a family man, having married Dorothie Hepworth in 1937 when he was 26; he also had a daughter Rita, and he did not like the idea of being continually away from home.

So that he could spend more time with Dorothie and Rita he decided to buy a business – almost any business, providing it had either a

manufacturing or a distributive base. He rejected the idea of buying a firm which made teapots and earthenware hot water bottles because it was in the Potteries, away from his beloved Yorkshire and instead plumped for Maynard & Field, a Longroyd Bridge firm of wholesale drysalters. The building was ramshackled and had a leaking roof and the firm sold bleach, salt, firewood, firelighters, and such things as turpentine and donkey-stones! However, when in 1957 the firm made a small loss he decided to once again make a change.

Across in Hull a group of large retailers was trying to cut out the middleman and deal direct with manufacturers by creating a co-operative, but the idea failed. Lawrence believed that if he opened a warehouse, kept large stocks of a very wide range of goods which small shopkeepers could come and collect and pay cash for, and then take back to their shops in their own vehicles, he would be able to get a good price from the suppliers. He was only looking for a profit margin of $2^{1}/_{2}$ per cent, rather than the 10 per cent other wholesalers sought; he knew he could succeed. Nevertheless, the shopkeepers were used to wholesalers calling on them and wondered who he thought he was to say 'Come and fetch 'em!' However, interest levels continued to be low, and he spent two weeks working eleven and twelve hours a day delivering leaflets to local retailers. It was Lawrence Batley who coined the phrase 'Cash and Carry'!

He opened the first warehouse in 1958 in a disused laundry at Sheepbridge, in Huddersfield – that first morning there were five cars on the car park when he opened; he felt sure success would be his and by the end of the year money seemed to just flow in. In those early days he kept his money in an OXO tin, and wrote invoices by hand, but the purchase of a cash register helped to at least reduce his stress levels a little. At first he did anything and everything – moved cartons, priced the goods, paid the wages, and also smoked 40 cigarettes a day! It was killing him – he suffered from asthma and developed two duodenal ulcers, but he has lived to see unbelievable success in so many different ways.

However, by 1962 the firm had acquired a new 20,000 sq ft warehouse in Leeds Road, in Huddersfield – Lawrence preferred to

Another new Cash & Carry, Nottingham 1998

describe it as 'a supermarket for the shopkeeper'. It cost all of £32,000, had adjustable racking, and all goods had to be supplied on pallets, which could then be moved by the Lansing Bagnall fork-lift truck. Already turnover had amounted to £750,000 and he anticipated sales reaching £1 million within the year! Possibly uniquely, he had a committee made up of five of his shrewdest customers who held a monthly meeting with the three directors, Lawrence Batley, Freddie Bullock and a Mr H Sanderson. These meetings were to discuss the interests of the customers, and any matters which might benefit the users of the warehouse.

Lawrence Batley (right) with the company managing director Len McCormick at the opening of Batley's new head office

In 1968 the company opened a 65,000 sq ft warehouse in Sheffield, which was later extended to 80,000 sq ft; in 1972 a 80,000 sq ft warehouse was opened in Bradford, and in 1977 a 84,000 sq ft warehouse was opened in Preston, before in June 1979 Doncaster's Travis Cash & Carry were brought into the Batley fold. Initially he had invested £1500 in his venture, but when it was floated on the stock exchange in 1972, Lawrence Batley immediately became a millionaire – the offer was 115 times oversubscribed. However, he and members of his family ensured that they retained a controlling share interest. In 1983 the company spent £4 million on a new warehouse at Birtley near Durham. Further outlets have been opened in Edinburgh, Manchester, Birmingham, Cleveland, Coventry, Liverpool, Nottingham, Cardiff, Glasgow, Stourton on the outskirts of Leeds, and at Southampton. By 1990 Batleys had a turnover of £400 million a year.

Although the company had been floated so successfully, Lawrence Batley decided it was safer as a private company, and as such he could better determine its future policy and growth. He

therefore bought back all the other shares, offering the shareholders very generous terms.

By 1978, when he was 67, he was still able to devote two or three mornings a week to the office, while spending more time on his sporting interests. In 1981 the first Lawrence Batley Golf Tournament was played on the St Ives course at Bingley, before it was moved two years later to the Belfry course and renamed the Classic. Over the years Lawrence Batley has played in various pro-am tournaments and partnered such great players as Lee Trevino and Arnold Palmer. Today the company sponsors the Seniors Tournament, which is held at the Fixby course at Huddersfield, and has attracted international players such as South Africa's Bobby Verwey. There are also the Lawrence Batley stand at the MacAlpine Stadium and the Lawrence Batley Playing Fields.

Art and opera lover Lawrence Batley received the OBE in 1991 for his support of the National Art Education Archive Centre at Bretton College. Huddersfield's 470 seater Lawrence Batley Civic Theatre also owes much to this man who provided the largest individual donation towards its building costs. His company annually gives away many thousands of pounds to support a wide range of charitable causes.

In 1999 a new headquarters building for the company was opened adjacent to the Stourton outlet by the 88 year old chairman – and appropriately called 'Lawrence Batley House'. Perhaps today, with 18 warehouses and a company worth £500m, he comes to the office less often than in past years, but he must surely look back with considerable pride and satisfaction on what he, at over 40 years old, started from scratch when he decided to have a career change!

David Tarn

BOLTON ABBEY ESTATE

The Bolton Abbey Estate came to the Cavendish family in the middle of the 18th century, through the marriage of Charlotte Elizabeth, the only surviving child of the 3rd Earl of Burlington, to the 4th Duke of Devonshire. However, our story starts long before that, for Bolton has been a distinct estate for about 1,000 years, the name 'Bolton' signifying an enclosure with a house, possibly the manor house of Edwin, a Saxon earl.

In 1120 Cecily, daughter of Robert de Romille who was the first Norman lord, and wife of William Meschin, established a church of regular canons of the order of St Augustine at Embsay. It was Alice, her daughter, who made possible their move to the more sheltered site at Bolton some 35 years later. She is said to have done this as an expression of sorrow at the death of her son, the Boy of Egremont, who died in the Strid, but this does not seem possible as his signature appears on a document drawn up on the foundation of the Priory. The canons followed a rule of poverty, chastity and obedience, and were also to give alms and provide hospitality to visitors, and serve as parish priests.

Bolton Priory came under the patronage of the Cliffords of Skipton Castle, but suffered from incursions by the Scots during the 14th century. By the time construction of the Great West Tower began in 1520, monastic power and wealth was already coming to an end.

A northern uprising against proposals for the dissolution of the monasteries, the Pilgrimage of Grace, was put down by the King's men and Bolton was surrendered to the Commissioners in 1539. At dissolution, the nave was walled off and this has become the present day parish church. The priory gateway also survived and became the core of Bolton Hall, which has been the Yorkshire home of the Duke of Devonshire since 1754. Stone from the ruins of the priory was

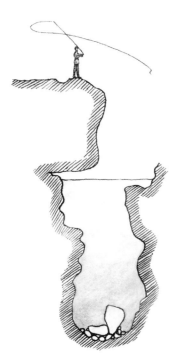

The Strid – where the River Wharfe surges through a narrow gorge – is the highspot for many visitors to the estate. It may look harmless but, at 30 feet deep, it is extremely dangerous. Anything which enters it rarely surfaces for several days.

used to build a grammar school, which later became the rectory.

Today the Priory Church is entered through the West Tower, but the window was not glazed nor a roof provided until the restorations of the 1980s – Christian worship has sanctified this place for almost 850 years!

The River Wharfe was originally crossed by a ferryboat a mile south of the priory. The Bolton Bridge known to many travellers for generations past was replaced during the 1990s by the modern bridge which now carries an increasing amount of traffic along the A59 from Skipton to Harrogate and beyond. The opening up of the Strid and much of the riverside and woodland to the public was encouraged by Rev William Carr, who was incumbent at the Priory and a close friend of the 6th Duke of Devonshire. Some 30 miles of paths were provided, stretching from Bolton Abbey up to Barden, and viewing points were created where seats were placed.

The estate covers 30,000 acres of some of the most beautiful countryside in the the Yorkshire Dales, about half of it being moorland, and is a much loved refuge for town and city dwellers at all seasons of the year. Throughout its length, the River Wharfe is a sparkling spectacle, dilatory in places, but dangerous where it narrows at the infamous Strid, a gorge where the water is up to 30 feet deep. Whilst human visitors may visit it for a day, the area is the permanent home for a rich and varied range of wildlife as well as being a busy, working estate.

At the beginning of the 20th century 100,000 tourists were travelling each year by train to the little railway station, which opened in the 1880s. In those early days special trains came from as far away as Sheffield, bringing people for a day in the countryside. From there they would walk across to the Cavendish Pavilion and waterside meadows, or make the steep climb to Simon's Seat.

The present Duke of Devonshire recalls coming to Bolton Abbey in 1926 when he was only six years old. King George V also arrived at the railway station, when he visited the estate as the guest of the present Duke's grandfather for the opening of the grouse season. The young boy was allowed to tell the King, on his return from the moors, that the England cricketers had regained the ashes – one longs for the day when that news can again be passed to the monarch!

Today, in addition to the tenanted farms and woodyard, there are other enterprises on the estate such as the Bunkbarn in the grounds of Barden Tower, with nearby Yorkshire Crafts in the old chapel, the village Post Office and cafe, and the Cavendish Pavilion which provides refreshments near to the river. The nearby memorial fountain commemorates the life of Lord Frederick Charles Cavendish, the son of William, the Seventh Duke of Devonshire. He was murdered in 1882 by 'The Invincibles' when he was the Chief Secretary of Ireland.

It is likely that from the earliest days some of the farm tenants also offered hostelry facilities to travellers along the old packhorse routes. Today that tradition is continued by the fine Devonshire Arms Country House Hotel, which offers quality hospitality to visitors. It was once known as the Burlington Arms, and when in 1792

George V arrives by train met by the 9th Duke of Devonshire

Lord Torrington stayed there he found the lodging excellent. His overnight stay, and a meal of mutton chops, salad, cold veal pie, as well as hay and corn for his horse, only cost him 4s 2$\frac{1}{2}$d!

In 1834 the hotel was extended and upgraded throughout. Later, in 1882, *Murray's Hand-Book for Yorkshire* tells us that 'The Devonshire Arms Hotel is a good Inn, usually charging hotel prices, and often full in season, but the proprietor finds rooms in the neighbourhood when this is the case'. We know that a few years later the hotel was tenanted to Joseph Speed, who also had the tenancy of one of the estate's farms. There were several inns on the estate which today are recalled in some of the farm names.

Today the Devonshire Arms Country House Hotel is one of the country's top hotels, complete with a leisure complex just across the road from the main site.

An Edwardian view of the Devonshire Arms

Below: left – the 9th Duke; right – the 10th Duke. Right: the present Duke and Duchess

HERBERT BROWN

Quality, New and Second Hand Jewellers and Pawnbrokers since 1840

John Brown was born in 1793 in Kingston upon Hull where he became a mariner and then a linen presser. However, at that time cities like Leeds and Sheffield were rapidly expanding as the industrial revolution gathered speed and, wanting to take advantage of this, John took his family to live in Leeds where he became a linen presser and outfitter. His son Charles Hood Brown was born in 1829.

Once in Leeds, John widened his business by also becoming a pawnbroker, and the company has one of its original pawn tickets dated 1838 which came from John's shop in Burley Road. Today the link between being an outfitter and a pawnbroker may seem strange, but in Victorian times many of the labouring classes were extremely poor and often had no money to pay for food for the next meal. The pawnbroker, who was commonly known as 'uncle', therefore held a very valuable position in society by providing cash, based on the pledging of some item of value by the client. As most poor people had no jewellery, watches, or other valuable items, they had to resort to placing in pawn articles such as the husband's best Sunday boots, waistcoats, overcoats, ladies' dresses, fire irons and fenders. When sheets or blankets were to be pledged they had to washed first! The most common pledges would be parcels of clothing, made up of shirts, underclothes and dresses. If a customer took in a suit he would be charged an extra 1d for hanging it up, or an extra 2d for wrapping it up in brown paper, with an extra 1/2d for the string! When necessary wives would even pawn their engagement or wedding rings to ensure there was food on the table; men would pawn silver watches, birds in cages, best walking sticks, pictures, clocks, house deeds and Herbert Brown's has even taken a horse and trap!

Charles joined his father in the business but he later combined trading as a pawnbroker with that of being a jeweller. By 1870 the business was trading as C Brown and had shops at 83 Burley Road, and at 20 Christopher Street in Leeds.

On a Monday morning it was a common sight to see queues stretching down the street from the

HERBERT BROWN,

The **LIBERAL CANDIDATE**,

By making a **X** in the square opposite the first name thus—

1	BROWN, HERBERT	X
2	Renton, A. F. G.	
3	Stamford, T. W.	

Do not sign your name.

Do not write your initials.

If you spoil your ballot paper, ask for another.

Please call before voting at the Liberal Committee Room, near the Polling Booth for your number.

Men voters on the Parliamentary Register can vote at this Election if not starred.

Women voters on the Parliamentary

General Election, Oct. 29th, 1924.

shop doorway, and these would usually last until lunchtime. In many instances one woman in each street would gather all her neighbours' pledge items, put them in a pram, sometimes towing a second one, and take them to the shop. The items would then be redeemed on a Friday evening after the customer had been paid his or her wages, so they could be worn over the weekend, before being pledged again on the following Monday.

Inside each of the early shops was a ladder which led to the first, second and sometimes third floors. On each floor a young lad, aged between 12 and 15, would be in charge of the parcels on his floor. On Mondays he stored the parcels away in number

An early photograph of the company's Middlesbrough branch (below), and (above) the Sheffield shop today

order and on Fridays passed them down a chute which led into the pledge office for handing out to the customers.

The shops were originally outfitting shops, rather than jewellery ones, and had only a small window displaying jewellery – hence the pictures of suits, coats and boots hanging outside the premises. Today, of the items pledged, 96 per cent are re-deemed; the remain-der are sold after a period of about eight months. The usual loan amount is 25 per cent of the item's original value, and the items that are sold are normally about half the original price.

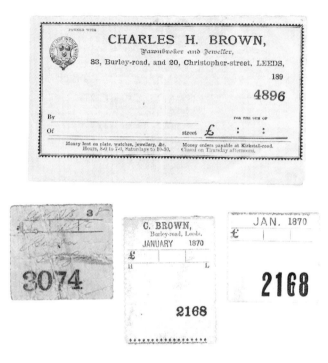

From the days of Charles Hood Brown the business has steadily expanded. Charles's son, Herbert Brown, who was born in 1863, had eight children. He was a very respected businessman, becoming the president of the Leeds Permanent Building Society, and a Leeds alderman. He not only expanded the business but also bought a woollen mill, which is still run by members of the Brown family today. However, on his death his business interests were divided between 27 members of the family!

His youngest son, who was born in 1909, was also called Herbert. After his father's death he borrowed money from the Midland Bank and bought back all the company shares from the rest of the family, but with the condition that the sale would not go through unless they all agreed. Once again it was a family business, but he had to sell off all but five of the shops to pay off the loan.

Herbert's son, Herbert Colin Brown, known as Colin, was born in 1936 and joined the firm in 1953. Together he and his father rebuilt the business and for the first time opened branches outside Leeds and Rotherham. Today Colin Brown is company chairman, and is assisted in the running of the business by four of his five sons, who are the sixth generation to enter the business – Simon, Michael, and twins Robert and Christopher are all directors. They have a staff of over 130 people who provide a knowledgeable service in jewellery and gifts, as well as a confidential and sensitive one to those who still come to pledge items.

Staff training is very important as most modern jewellery is valued on its gold content, whereas antique jewellery and diamond rings are valued according to a different set of criteria. Managers and staff must have an expert knowledge of their subject, and be aware of the latest technology which can prevent them accepting fake diamonds and other precious stones, and counterfeit Rolex watches and similar expensive brands.

Herbert Brown now has 18 shops, including two in London, and six franchises, and anticipates further expansion in the future. It is still a private family company, but believes it offers a service of a special nature which enables it to compete with much larger companies.

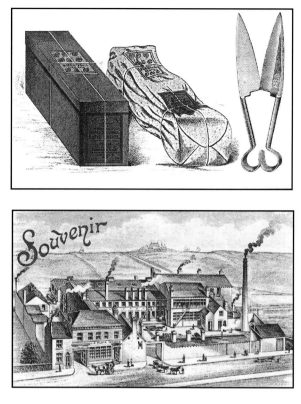

Back in 1730 William Wilkinson and his sons Robert and Longley started to manufacture shears, scissors and knives at Spring Works in Grimesthorpe Road, Sheffield – it overlooked the Don Valley where so much industrial development would take place in the next century. The business prospered and by 1889 it had become a public company, William Wilkinson Ltd.

However, in about 1865 Charles Burgon, a cutler from the Philadelphia district of Sheffield, saw the potential in a sheep shear patented by James Ball and they formed a partnership in 1870; Ball left the company in 1883. Charles Burgon died in 1894 and in 1896 Harry Burgon, one of two sons who inherited the Burgon & Ball Sheep Shearing Manufacturing Company, invested some money in Wilkinson Ltd, and it became Burgon & Wilkinson.

Burgon & Ball had been based at La Plata Works at Malin Bridge since 1873 where the river gave it its water power. Later steam engines were installed, to be succeeded in the 20th century by electricity. They had successfully marketed a new sheep shearing machine in Australia and South America – its working principles are still used today. Agencies, with sales and service crews, were established throughout Australia and South America, but the cost was enormous and put great strain on the company. As a result of this, and the way Charles had

also left equal shares to his two sons, the forming of a public company was inevitable, and was the only way forward.

Burgon & Ball Ltd was formed in 1898 with a share capital of £40,000, Charles's son Frederic becoming managing director. However, within twelve months they had bought Burgon & Wilkinson, which gave them an entry into the American market. Sadly Frederic died two years after becoming managing director and was succeeded by Benjamin Hinds, who had been with the firm since the formation of the limited company.

Benjamin Hinds was a very enthusiastic

"BURGON 1901 MODEL."

PRICE,   50s.

The "DAISY."

motorist and is thought to have been only the third person in Sheffield to own a car. It was about this time that the company imported cars from France, these being shipped from various French ports before being transported by rail to Sheffield. The name(s) of the manufacturers is unknown but they were 'branded' at Sheffield with such names as 'La Plata', 'Talbots', 'Decauvilles' and a 'Darracq'. The company's involvement with the motor trade continued for many years, and Benjamin Hinds remained as managing director until 1938.

In 1894 a group of Sheffield workers formed a sheep shearing manufacturing company, and with local labour leaders and the Sheep Shearers' Union of Australia formed the Trade Unionists' Sheep Shear Co-operative. It survived until the 1960s when it was bought out by Burgon & Ball. Today its workforce includes ALL eleven members of the Wool Shear Workers' Union – the smallest and one of the oldest affiliated trade unions in this country!

In 1918 Burgon & Ball had bought out Rowland Brindley's hammer manufacturing company at Bramall Lane for £2,500, and transferred its activities to Malin Bridge. Within two years garden shear production had outstripped that of sheep shears and the company was becoming more versatile in the engineering work that it took on for local firms.

With the outbreak of the Second World War, the company tooled up for the war effort. After that it decided not to re-enter

The grinding shop circa 1930s

THE "**LAPLATA**" **HORSE CLIPPER.**

THIS is all one desires, and can be worked in conjunction with the "BURGON" Sheep Shearer.

This Machine is Noiseless.

Cheaper Machines can be obtained.

All parts are interchangeable, and made of the Best Sheffield Steel by the best Sheffield Workmen. Thousands in use everywhere.

All Machines are fitted with the Burgon's Patent Grinder.

See Illustration on opposite page.

the mechanical shearing market, giving other firms a clear run, but enabling it to concentrate on its specialist hand sheep shears.

A new forge and a new despatch warehouse were completed in 1974 and further investment has followed over the years. In the 1980s there were various takeovers; and the Falklands War cost it export sales to South America.

In 1988 the company was sold to the Newship Group, but it decided to divest itself of what it saw as the peripheral business, which included sheep shear manufacturing. The present owners bought the sheep shearing and tool manufacturing business and with it the name, Burgon & Ball. In 1991 they added to the business the scythe manufacturers, Tyzack Sons & Turner.

As sheep fleeces vary with the breed – some are short and wiry, others long and soft – so the design of shears also varies. The shears are cut from 4in wide coils of steel. The steel goes through no less than 22 stages – from heating and shaping, to hardening and grinding, and finally to sharpening and setting the tension and cut. Individual countries want their own unique design, whether the shears vary from long blades to short blades, or have a different tension on the blades; the company has 50 separate patterns!

As we enter another century, Burgon & Ball and its 30 workers still supply a wide range of

A shearing machine circa 1900

sheep shears, garden and builders tools. Now the emphasis has changed towards items for the gardener, including an extensive range of knives, various tools and ornamental products.

A hundred years ago there were eight sheep shear manufacturers in this country; Burgon & Ball Ltd alone remains – 'Shear Excellence Since 1730'.

They export much of their production to countries as varied as Uruguay, Argentina, Australia, New Zealand, South Africa and North America. Their reputation as manufacturers of sheep shears is still second to none – although in this country these may also be used to trim topiary or carpet beds!

caldene

Deep among the Pennine hills George Thomas Uttley was born in Hebden Bridge in 1898. He attended the local school and started work in the clothing trade at the age of 13.

When he was called up in 1917 he joined the London Rifles, and was subsequently wounded in France, but in 1919 he returned to the clothing industry in his home town.

In 1922 George, along with his two brothers-in-law Jack and Walter Lord, formed the Caldene Clothing Company – each partner providing £15 capital. Soon the business was transferred to a former army hut.

The mills in the Calder Valley – hence their choice of name – have long had a good reputation for weaving hard-wearing cloths such as corduroy, Bedford cord, Cavalry twill and Derby tweeds and the local clothing industry produced hard-wearing clothes for manual workers.

The Princess Royal meets four generations of Uttleys in 1991

From the beginning George Uttley concentrated on making breeches for farmers and agricultural workers, which were normally worn with leggings or long stockings. The early trade was solely mail order, the customer writing in and asking for cloth patterns, a style booklet, and a self measurement form, which they later returned with choice of cloth, measurements and money.

In those early days wives and daughters helped with the sewing, but as the orders increased so did the workforce, and in 1936 the firm opened a small factory in nearby Mytholmroyd, the nucleus of today's business.

George's son Kenneth joined the business in 1936, but in 1941 he volunteered to join the Royal Air Force. During the war the company mainly produced motorcyclists' pantaloons for army despatch riders, and breeches for the women of the land army.

After the war Caldene changed from its pre-war mail order trade to supplying ready-to-wear breeches and jodhpurs for distribution to shops and stores. In the early 1960s it introduced the 'Cotswold' and 'Pacemaker' one-way stretch jodhpurs, which were made from cloth designed for ski wear which had a warp stretch.

Joining the company in 1967 was Carl Uttley, a third generation member of the family who had previously studied as a production engineer at Leeds College of Clothing Technology.

The early 1970s saw the introduction of two-way stretch jodhpurs made from nylon/Lycra fabrics. Other additions to the range at this time were jackets and hunt coats. At the end of the decade the company pioneered the 'Cavalier' range of thermal garments from a cloth which had a cotton backing.

Subsequent developments have included gamekeeper suits, mounted-police breeches, chauffeurs' suits, breeches for films, and even sets of racing leathers for riders in the Isle of Man TT races. Harvey Smith, the famous showjumper, has also been a customer.

The first export order was made to Canada in 1963, and since then Caldene has sent its specialist clothing to many parts of the world, including Europe, Japan, Australia and South Africa. Another innovative product is a ladies' riding habit, officially approved by the Side Saddle Association.

In November 1991 four generations of the Uttley family were presented to HRH The Princess Royal, much to the delight of great grandfather George.

More recently the company has devised a unique way of trading on the Internet, while maintaining faith with their hundreds of stockists nationwide.

The factory has been extended six times over the years, and this family-owned business continues to meet the needs of a niche market, but always looking out for related innovations which will broaden its range of customers.

CALMON

Hanns Herman Calmon was born in Berlin in 1913. From an early age he showed an artistic eye and an appreciation of design, colour and style – as well as an interest in textiles. On leaving school he took a two year apprenticeship with Gebrueder Simon in Berlin, before studying at Roubaix, at the heart of the French textile trade.

In the 1930s he came to England where he began a business with his close friend and best man, John Elton; it was linked to the brewing industry and the importing of hops from the Balkans! However, the outbreak of war brought an end to this venture and he joined the

Hanns Calmon

Pioneer Corps. After the liberation of Belgium he was posted to Brussels, where his parents had been hiding throughout the hostilities, and now he was able to help them.

When the war ended he took a postgraduate degree in textiles at Leeds University, after which he became a 'middle man' – 'a manufacturer without looms' – a person who got others to produce fabrics for him on theirs. He had found a niche in the market, but before long some of his best customers, the multiple tailors, saw opportunities for cutting out such middlemen, and either dealt direct with the weavers or set up their own production unit. This cut out Hanns and he had to find another way forward.

Joe Lyons, a business associate who worked for John Collier in Leeds, mentioned to Hanns the difficulty of getting woven labels for their garments, there being only one British supplier, a firm based in Coventry. Hanns had a real feel for business, he saw an opening and took it!

Hanns Calmon was a man of true principle – he never kept suppliers waiting for their money, he never let his standards fall, he avoided debt and was content to let his business grow without overstretching the resources. He believed his workforce should be multi-skilled; he felt it was good for them, because doing a variety of tasks prevented tedium, and it also ensured he always had cover in times of staff shortage. Sometimes his views bordered on eccentricity, but he never saw the need to be at the cutting edge of technology. He did not see new technology as a means to cutting staff, rather that new pieces of equipment increased production and provided the need to increase staff.

The Calmon family business, Saxony, 1920

In his personal life Hanns was a non-smoker, took only an occasional glass of wine or beer and never had a television. And, whilst not a gardener, he admired the work of others who were. He had no edge, but although rather shy, mixed well with celebrities and ordinary people alike.

His wife Jadwiga, whilst taking no part in the running of the business, was respected by members of the workforce for she was concerned for their welfare and that of their families. She was the daughter of a Warsaw doctor, a beautiful aristocratic lady, refined and well-educated, speaking several languages.

Hanns was a man of compassion, and whilst perhaps often giving a sense of being rather sober, actually had a good sense of humour. Although he could drive, he chose not to do so and therefore

Above: Becks Mill, Silsden
Below: Rhone Shed, Cabbage Mills

Top: erection of the first loom in Silsden, 1952
Above: Marcus Lee operating a needle loom, 1986

had to have his offices near to Forster Square Railway Station in Bradford, from where he could readily catch a train to business associates in either Leeds or London, and to his factory in Keighley.

In choosing Keighley, Hanns Calmon came to the heart of the West Riding textile industry, an industry based on the quality and abundance of water. Back in 1876 there were 23 cotton mills in the town, and at one point 70 manufacturers were engaged in a broad range of related trades. Becks Mill at Silsden, a few miles away from Keighley, was a very suitable building: local people were already skilled at Jacquard weaving, and it was not far from Steeton railway station so Hanns could leave his bicycle there when making journeys further afield!

Being an immigrant he was aware of the plight of displaced persons from mainland Europe,

A selection of early labels, circa late 1950s

many of whom arrived in the area in the 1950s and he therefore advertised in the London-based Ukrainian newspaper *Thor*. He brought his first two looms from Wuppertal in Germany, but while customers waited for his garment labels, he could not persuade his equipment to work. The delay nearly killed the firm before it started production, and in one year they had a loss of £4,000 – no small amount in those days.

However, the business expanded in 1952, through the production of Coronation woven bookmarks – an ideal promotional product, and soon there were 12 looms working three shifts, giving 24 hour continuous working.

By 1961 the company had outgrown its Silsden premises and moved to Cabbage Mills in Keighley where they had 20 Vaupel shuttle looms and 35 employees. Three years later, 22 year old Tony Lee joined them as a designer – he became regarded as a versatile first lieutenant.

Year by year turnover grew by about 8 per cent, and by 1971 it had reached £150,000, and was fast catching up on its sole British competitor.

That year Hanns bought Heaton & Flint's iron foundry and an adjacent quarry for £8,500, and Tony was given the job of building a new shed to house the 30 looms – he quickly became quantity surveyor, structural engineer, site foreman and general factotum!

Tony Lee didn't come from a design or engineering background – his parents had a

milk-round business in Yeadon; perhaps that's where he gained those first managerial lessons and realised that you have to get on with the job whatever the circumstances. When he left school he got a job as a weft-lad at James Ives & Co in Yeadon where he worked alongside two parolees from Wakefield Gaol, neither of whom could read or write, and he became their book-keeper. Soon he joined a design course at Bradford Technical College where he gained his City & Guilds examinations, and then went on to take higher qualifications. Hanns Calmon had moved his career along for him, but now with the completion of the shed, which coincided with the company's silver jubilee, he felt it was also time to move on. Tony Lee was 30 years old and married with two children, and so he

Products from the printing division which was acquired in 1994

Calmon labels and badges from the 1960s up to the present day

departed to further his career in America.

America gave him the chance to work on a wider range of fabrics, with better design and modern technological facilities and more customer contact – he grew in self-confidence and self-esteem, and in staff management skills. At the Weave Corporation he learned much that he was able to bring back to Britain, and in particular to Calmon & Co.

Domestic circumstances brought Tony Lee back to his own country in 1975, and to Calmon's. He wasn't sure if this was the place to be, but gradually he used his American experiences, and persuaded Hanns Calmon to move the administration from Bradford to above the factory at Keighley.

However, Hanns Calmon was now a sick man and his illness was taking a more

serious turn; Tony visited him at his sickbed in London each week, bringing him news of the company's progress. Tony Lee was given the opportunity to take over the company – with the proviso that he take care of Mrs Calmon; Hanns might regard him as his protege, but still Tony had much to consider. The company had enjoyed 25 years success, but now much of the machinery was old and behind the times – even the balance sheet was not good. Once again he looked back to his time in America, and as his first modest investment chose some electronic card-punching equipment – but if it was the wrong decision it might mean bankruptcy.

Hanns Calmon later had to have surgery for a brain tumour and following a recurrence of the problem he died in 1979; he was only 66.

However, fate seemed to be on Tony's

Tony Lee, Chairman   *The Parkwood Street premises built in 1971-72*

side, for having decided to buy four new broad looms, each capable of producing six times the output of the old ones, a new customer came on the scene.

Mike Leonard came from Colne, in Lancashire, and he sold pop badges – the names Led Zeppelin and Iron Maiden took on a completely new meaning as Calmon's designed and produced 50,000 badges a week! Tony knew that he had to keep these looms working full-time if the company was to remain viable; this work would make that possible. It also meant the creation of complex designs to short deadlines; it demanded a review of working practices – they had to prove themselves good enough for the job! The answer had to be 'YES'. Tony invested in a CAD (computer aided design) system – Calmon was one of the first companies in the country to install one. Keeping up with new technology in this way led to increased sales and staffing levels – the old Calmon policy. The change from shuttle looms to modern equipment was a phased process; it only occurred when one of the senior weavers reached retirement – again it was part of

the Calmon philosophy: people matter.

Calmon Ferreira was formed in 1988, following which a new 20,000 square foot building was bought and equipped with ten new computerised weaving machines, and staffed by local people. This was the blueprint for future international expansion.

In the early 1990s a partnership was formed with Robert Kaliner of New York, and together, Tony Lee and Robert Kaliner rapidly established partnerships in the Dominican Republic, Ireland, India, the Far East and New York itself.

Year upon year Calmon has invested heavily in modern equipment which is at the forefront of technological developments. This has included broad cloth looms dedicated to the manufacture of tie material, fine dress cloths, furnishing fabrics and cashmere luxury fabrics, as well as Air Jet broadlooms for label weaving, and computer aided Jacquard design systems. Today they have 14 designers and the investment for the year 2000 was projected at about £3 million.

The company is now the largest woven-label company in the United Kingdom, with the capacity to manufacture 9 million labels a week. Orders have even included badges for the 1986 NASA Moonshot crew, as well as uniform badges for the team manufacturing the rocket and its support functions.

George Hollingbery's parents were publicans in London, and he was born in 1903. Sadly his father died when George was still a lad and his mother married again. She worked hard to bring money into the home, but his stepfather could dispose of it as quickly as she earned it, and so when George came of age there was nothing left.

George felt the future lay in things electric. He got a job as the sales representative for the north of the country with Exide, selling accumulators to provide power to early radios, or as we used to call them 'wirelesses'. However, he became friendly with Walter Honor, a dealer in Hull, and started a service to customers where they hired out accumulators and recharged them as necessary, calling the business Comet Battery Services Ltd; it was run

George Hollingbery

from small premises in Wincolmlee, Hull where they eventually also sold and hired the receivers. When the wireless sets started to be powered by mains electricity, and accumulators were no longer needed, they changed the name of the firm

to Comet Radio Services Ltd. As the business grew, the firm moved premises to Jameson Street and finally to 48 and 50 George Street.

Anticipating the outbreak of the Second World War they gathered together a massive stock of spare parts, but in April 1941 a bomb landed on the George Street premises which were completely destroyed, the force of the explosion casting some of the radio receivers onto the canopy of the nearby Dorchester Cinema. However, a prefabricated building was erected on the site, from which they traded until 1955. It had been a wise move to concentrate on renting radios, for during the war years there were no new radios for the public to buy. During the war George served in the RAF Volunteer Reserve and Walter on war work, connected with submarines.

In 1951 television came to the West Riding with the opening of the Holme Moss transmitter and so Comet changed its name again, to Comet Radiovision Services Ltd. At that time the only working directors and shareholders were George and Molly Hollingbery.

1941: Despite Hitler's bombs it's soon business as usual

It was also in that year that their son Michael joined the firm, straight from school, where he told me he 'had failed everything'! However, he worked his way through the company gaining a good knowledge of all aspects of it.

In 1956 Comet made £42,000 profit from £142,000 of sales. Sadly George collapsed and died in London in 1958 while attending a meeting. Molly and Michael, who was still in his early twenties, overnight became joint managing directors.

George had not been keen on the idea of hiring out televisions; but Michael was. However, by then they were rather late into the game and there was tremendous competition offering low weekly payments from the big players who had enormous capital with which to fund their projects. Nevertheless, Michael worked out that if they could get some very reliable sets they could be retailed from the shops and thereby bring the overheads down to nil. He entered into discussion with Phillips and convinced them that the number of sets he would need would grow

*Interior and exterior displays
circa late 40s early 50s*

considerably, and therefore in return he wanted a good discount, which he got. They already had an enviable reputation for after-sales service, and they financed all their own rental and hire purchase arrangements.

The rental idea worked, and soon Comet was enjoying a great increase in the number of customers, which meant it could extend its range of models to offer better customer choice. The first branch was opened in Bridlington – on 5 November 1960 – only £1500 was spent on the conversion. In the next five years others followed at Driffield, Goole, Doncaster, Wakefield and Pontefract, each with its own service department. Whilst he was renting sets to the public, Michael made it a general rule that the company should own its premises. In 1968 it bought

Harold Child's business in Leeds, which also dealt with general electrical stock, and this gave Comet experience in handling washing machines.

The abolition of retail price control by Ted Heath was a matter of real concern, for Michael Hollingbery was worried that their prices would be undercut.

He therefore decided to open a discount warehouse – it opened in a Hull warehouse and was an instant flop! Back at the drawing board it was soon realised that the problem lay in lack of effective advertising; they had to invest in full page advertisements which clearly spelt out the price of each item.

On his way to the opening of the warehouse in Leeds in 1969, Michael,who was returning from a shooting expedition, saw a lot of people going in the direction of Armley where the discount outlet was based. He remarked to his dog that he hoped they were all going to Comet – and they were! The company's solicitors were then asked to find similar old warehouses, and soon there were Comet discount warehouses in Stockton on Tees and also in Edinburgh.

In 1972 it was time to go public – in 1962 its profits had been £23,000, in 1970 £117,000, in 1971 £340,000, and by the first six months of 1972 they had risen to a staggering £718,000. At this time Comet had nine discount warehouses with a further ten in the process of being developed. All the stock was in cartons; it wasn't until 1975 that it was decided to convert the Birmingham warehouse and start displaying the goods – that decision brought an almost instant 25 per cent increase in sales and was soon taken up at the other outlets.

Michael was keen that all customers should have long term peace of mind, and therefore negotiated with Prudential a scheme for a 5 year warranty; however, there was also £20 profit on each one sold!

In 1984 Comet was taken over by Kingfisher plc in a £189 million deal.

In 1991 the company opened its first service headquarters in Leeds and two years later began to reposition the chain as a purely out of town retailer.

Comet Group plc launched The Comet Price Index in 1995 to reinforce the company's commitment to price, each day updating its information on Channel 4 Teletext. In 1999 the company launched the Every Day Low Price strategy to underpin its proposition of offering customers consistently low prices. As part of this, Comet does not have seasonal sales or trade-ins. In the same year, the company also went on-line with fully transactional trading on the net, teaming up with *The Sun*'s CurrantBun.com to provide customers with free internet access.

By 1996 Comet Group plc's number of stores had risen to 250, and three years later it recorded profits of £33.4 million from sales of £862 million.

But why the name Comet? – Back in those early days a friend of George Hollingbery in Bradford owned a company called Comet Battery Services and he let George use the name. That was named after the Comet pub at Hatfield, near to where the original Comet aircraft was developed, the precursor of the famous Mosquito bomber.

R R DONNELLEY & SONS

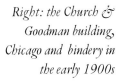

Our story begins in Hull in 1787 when George Prince first published the *Hull Packet* newspaper. Over the years it changed hands several times but in 1831 was taken over by partners William Roger Goddard and Robert Brown. When they dissolved their partnership in 1838 William Goddard set up an opposition newspaper called the *Hull & East Riding Times*.

In 1841 he ceased newspaper publishing but remained a jobbing printer. Five years later John William Lancaster became his partner and infused new life into the business, and a branch was opened at 19 Bridge Street, York in 1854. However, when they decided to terminate this partnership in 1858 John Lancaster kept the York premises.

John set up as a Wholesale and Retail Law Stationer, Account Book Manufacturer, Printer, Lithographer and Engraver, etc at the Blue Bell Yard factory, a five storey building. He now engaged 28 year old Ben Johnson, who came from Huddersfield, to take control of his printing and stationery business; Ben had served an apprenticeship to an engraver.

When John Lancaster died in 1867, aged 46, Ben Johnson and a Mr Tessyman bought the business. Due to its growth, it was decided to build a new factory in Micklegate in 1872, but while overseeing the building works in cold weather, Mr Tessyman contracted pneumonia and died.

By 1880 Ben Johnson was the sole owner and the firm became Ben Johnson & Co. On several occasions it proved necessary to extend the Micklegate factory, the last being in 1907 when it reached a total of 75,000 sq. ft.

R R Donnelley

Ben Johnson

Right: the Church & Goodman building, Chicago and bindery in the early 1900s

Left: machine room in the early 1900s and J W Lancaster printing offices, Hull

Ben Johnson died in 1901, aged 71. His obituary tells us that he had been very involved with the British Association, and had been with them to visit Canada some years earlier. He had also been vice-chairman of the Ebor Building Society, as well as being involved with some local trusts.

His sons Cecil and Gilbert now took control of the business and in 1910 it became a private limited liability company. Both directors made extensive visits to Europe and the United States looking at the latest production methods, and frequently as a result introduced new equipment to their own factory. At that time their work consisted largely of printing guide books, railway timetables and wrappers and labels for Rowntrees.

Unfortunately in 1932 a large fire destroyed the mainly wooden factory premises and therefore a new factory – the present one – was built in Boroughbridge Road. However it was only 57,500 sq ft, smaller than the one that had been destroyed, and rationalisation of production was required. Many of the old products were discontinued and emphasis was placed on quality colour printing of travel brochures, catalogues, guidebooks, and wrappers and labels – the client list included such well known companies as Rowntrees, Terry's of York, Cunard, Imperial Airways, BSA, Daimler, and Ford.

During the years of the Second World War the RAF occupied half the factory, and with a much reduced work force Gilbert Johnson kept the business going. After the war Ben Johnson & Co Ltd attracted many new customers, and larger contracts, including printing football pools coupons for Vernons, carrying out work for Procter & Gamble, and Meccano, as well as producing many magazine covers and inserts. Since before the war the company had seen that the future was in off-set lithograph printing, and therefore was ahead of many of its competitors.

Following the death of Cecil Johnson, his son Bernard joined his uncle in control of the family firm. As new extensions came on stream the company developed into binding and also produced cartons. On the death of Gilbert Johnson in 1968 Bernard Johnson assumed full control of the business, by now one of the largest family-owned printing companies in the United Kingdom. In 1975 their first web fed press was installed, which along with new binding equipment enabled it to speed up production of its publications.

In 1978 Bernard Johnson died – it was the end of an era – the Johnson family had controlled the business for 120 years!

The business now became part of R R Donnelley & Sons Ltd of Chicago in the United States. This was also a long-established family business having been founded about a hundred years earlier. Richard Robert Donnelley had been a journeyman printer in Canada before he joined the printing and publishing partnership of Church & Goodman, which then became Church, Goodman & Donnelley. In 1870 it was renamed the Lakeside Publishing and Printing Company, but the following year in the great Chicago fire its newly constructed plant was destroyed.

A new factory was built on the same site but difficult trading conditions over the next decade brought several changes of partners, and company names. In 1880 Richard Donnelley formed the Chicago Directory Company which published the first Chicago City Directory, listing business names and addresses; it was the first of many such listings to be published by them. In 1886 the firm secured its first contract to print

Top right: Donnelley's Chicago manufacturing division and corporate building and (above) the York premises

telephone directories for the Chicago Telephone Co. The following year R R Donnelley's eldest son became head of the Chicago Directory Company.

Over the next 30 years these two companies saw great growth, which included producing the *Encyclopaedia Britannica* in 1910. In 1916 the Reuben H Donnelley Corporation was formed to publish telephone directories.

Today the two Donnelley companies are not connected, although one prints many of the items that the other publishes. In 1927 R R Donnelley started to print mass circulation magazines, such as *Time*, and 20 years later also the printing and binding of *Life*.

Following its acquisition of Ben Johnson in 1978, Donnelley's put a satellite network in place to transmit data between the United Kingdom and the United States. In America R R Donnelley contract prints several Sunday magazines, and from 1996 has produced the *Reader's Digest*.

Back in York the company now produces BT telephone directories and also Yellow Pages telephone directories, not just for Britain but also for some European countries as well. Shortly the company will once again be on the move, this time to occupy large premises near to Knaresborough, and adjacent to the junction with the A1 trunk road.

Drummond

DRUMMOND GROUP PLC

James Drummond was born in Blyth, Northumberland in 1819 and came to Bradford when he was a child. After leaving school he went to work for a firm of worsted manufacturers called Hill & Smith. Having gained much experience and also shown his abilities he was eventually made a partner and the firm became Hill, Smith & Drummond. James took over the active management of the business and soon they needed to expand into larger premises and took over a part of Lister's old mills at Manningham, Bradford, in 1849. Mr Smith retired in 1851 and James also bought out Mr Hill's interest in the company. The business

James Drummond

continued to expand and in 1856 he began to build a mill at Lumb Lane. By 1870 it housed 45,000 spindles which supplied yarn to 300 looms in the weaving shed – a very significant capacity even by modern standards. The firm also supplied many other local manufacturers with yarn as well as exporting considerable amounts. In 1872 the name of the business was changed to James Drummond & Sons.

Eventually the Levi and Selka families became major shareholders in what was still a private company.

In 1924 the company exhibited at the British Empire Exhibition in London, and in the commemorative brochure they tell how at that time 'greasy wool' was imported direct from Australia, New Zealand and South Africa. On arrival the bales of wool were broken and the wool combed to separate the short fibres (noils) from the longer ones (tops). The tops were put through various machines to straighten the fibres and to form 'roving' from which yarn

Lumb Lane Mills, Bradford

could be spun. The roving then passed through various rollers to make the thread thinner. Yarn is either a single thread, or two or more twisted together to give more strength.

Before the yarn could be woven into cloth it was necessary to prepare a 'warp' – the individual threads being transferred into a broad 'web' which could then be wound on a beam ready for the loom. In the case of 'fancies' the different coloured threads were arranged in a given order to produce a pattern, and on the loom were crossed with 'weft' to form a cloth.

After weaving any defects were removed by the burlers and the menders before the cloth was dyed or finished. At that time much of the finished cloth was exported to North and South America, all parts of Europe, various parts of the British Empire and to the Far East.

James Drummond & Sons Ltd became a public limited company in 1958. Over the years the company had become recognised as specialists in the spinning and weaving of high quality worsted fabrics, mainly for menswear, much of it being exported to the Middle and Far East and to North America.

The Drummond Group was formed in 1973, following the merger of James Drummond & Sons Ltd and Stroud Riley & Co Ltd. Prior to 1977 about 70 per

Company motor transport in the early 1920s

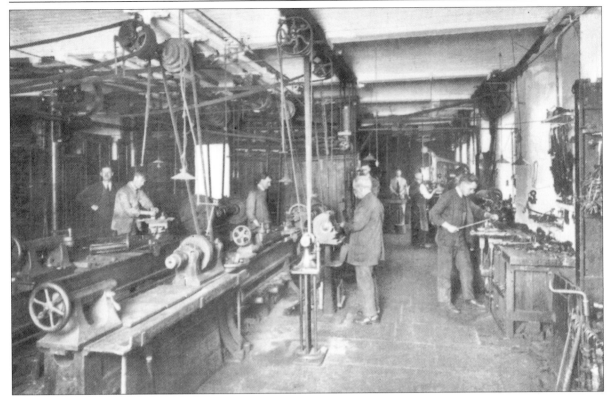

General view of the mechanics shop in the 1920s

cent of its production was exported to the Middle East but when that market collapsed the company decided to concentrate on long run worsted production aimed at both men and women's British high street multiple retail chains, as well as at uniform and career wear, particularly for financial institutions.

In 1979 a majority interest in the company was sold to Stefan Simmonds, who became chief executive and later chairman. In the following two years Atomik Mohairs Ltd, specialist worsted exporters, and James Haywood & Sons, the worsted operation of Tootal Ltd, were added to the group. In 1983 Longbottoms (Sowerby Bridge) Ltd, specialist manufacturers of uniform cloth, were acquired and in 1986 the world famous company, Salts (Saltaire) Ltd, joined the group and were relocated into Drummond Mill. A further purchase was made in 1990 – John Crowther & Sons (Milnbridge) Ltd, the largest vertically integrated woollen cloth manufacturer in the United Kingdom, also came into the fold.

Today the James Drummond Group is the largest manufacturer of worsted apparel fabric in the United Kingdom.

the Ecology
Building Society

The Ecology Building Society is a very young society compared to many of the larger names we know and have known on our high streets. Whilst it is very definitely a complete building society as is required by the various Acts of Parliament, it is very different from the others.

The Society came into being following a discussion between friends at the Party Conference of the Ecology Party (now the Green Party) in 1980. David Pedley, a solicitor based in Cross Hills, near Keighley, told how he was wanting to buy a dilapidated property with some adjoining land, but was finding it almost impossible to obtain a mortgage on it. Eventually the conversation moved to the point where someone said 'we ought to start our own society' – and so they did!

At that time it was possible to start a building society with a mere £5000 – today you would need to accumulate £1 million! Ten friends, the initial investors, provided £500 each. Further reserves were later required and a group of Foundation Shareholders had to invest a total of £90,000, not knowing when or if they would get their money back.

The Society started trading from an office above business premises in Cross Hills in March 1981, with David Pedley splitting his time

Projects in which the Society has been involved include a barn conversion (before and after shots below left) and a house built with recycled materials (below right)

between his solicitor's practice and this embryo building society. As would be expected, it grew quite slowly, but steadily. When it was known it had given its first mortgage, both borrowers and investors started showing much greater interest in this alternative, niche player.

David sought advice on applications for mortgages on smallholdings, which formed a high proportion of mortgage requests at that time, from Gus Smith, whom he had met through their involvement with organic farms. Gus became a director in 1983 and is now the Society's chairman. In 1985 Bob Lowman was appointed chief executive on David Pedley's departure, and was succeeded by Paul Ellis in 1995. Paul had joined the board in 1984 as a non-executive director.

Today the range of mortgages provided covers a much wider range of properties, both urban and rural, many of which are in need of renovation.

The Society works closely with housing associations and housing co-operatives. Some of these groups buy up terraced properties which can then be let to people who might otherwise be homeless, while other groups are seeking to follow a certain community lifestyle. At Nenthead in Cumbria, it worked with local people to enable them to revive and sustain what might have been a dying community, protecting the viability of the village school and post office, when no other lenders wanted to know. Today it is a thriving community with a new lead mining museum. At Fawcett Mills, near Tebay, a totally derelict old water mill was rebuilt by two women who took it over, with the Ecology Building Society's help. Today it is run as a conference/ holiday centre for disabled people.

The Society is happy to help people carry through 'do-it-yourself' projects, especially where they use reclaimed local stone, brick and slates and other second-hand materials. As the work proceeds the borrowers can return to the Society for further advances. Their policy has always been to charge such advances at the standard rate, whereas other lenders traditionally charged higher rates.

The Ecology Building Society is against indiscriminate new building which uses up green-field sites, preferring to see ecologically sound buildings erected on brown-field sites – that is buildings with good energy efficiency, using natural materials and local labour. It likes to talk to borrowers about their ideas, pointing would-be clients to people who are experts in a range of environmentally friendly solutions. Over recent years the Society has co-operated in a number of exciting new building schemes in places as far apart as Scotland and Sussex.

The Building Societies Act of 1986 has brought in new areas of compliance, and the Society has had to continually lift its levels of reserves. Throughout the past twenty years the Foundation Shareholders' contribution has been invaluable, and they have been tremendous friends who have ensured that those initial ideas and principles have been carried forward. It is a truly mutual society which cares about individuals. It has savers who are not simply wanting a high rate of interest on their money but who have an agenda of support for sustainability and community.

Today the Society has about 640 mortgagees, but it is also taking in record levels of investment month by month. Whilst it may lend on only about 140 properties a year, a sum of about £7 million, it offers hope to people who want to preserve our heritage, who want to show a concern for 'mother earth', and it still occupies a niche place in the building society movement.

It has plans to build a new headquarters on some wasteland in nearby Silsden, using those same principles it encourages others to use, and also protecting the jobs of local staff who have served the Society over the years.

FORTUNE'S WHITBY KIPPERS

William Fortune founded his kippering business in Whitby in 1872. Today it is still run by his family, now in the care of two of his great-great-grandsons, Barry and Derek Brown. Derek joined his Uncle Bill, a former Naval seaman and a great-grandson of the founder, as a partner in 1990 and Barry, who had been a steel erector, bought out his uncle's share in 1994.

Originally the family used to live adjacent to the small shop and smokehouse, in narrow Henrietta Street, not many yards away from the cliff face and the sea. Not much changes in that part of Whitby – the premises have altered but little, as have the curing methods used.

In those Victorian days, and up until about 1976, the herrings were mainly caught locally, although some came from the Irish Sea and Scotland when Whitby herrings were not available.

The gutted herrings are soaked in brine for about 40 minutes before being 'pricked' (poked through the shoulder) onto tenterhooks on 5 foot long bars and hung up in the smokehouse, 300-400 herrings at a batch. The fish hang there for between 18-24 hours, over an open fire of beech and oak wood shavings, sawdust and chippings which is lit on the smokehouse floor; however, care is needed, for too much smoking makes them dry. It is a continuous process, the ones on the lower rows, nearest the fire, being removed first and the others then being moved down.

Ellen Fortune outside the shop in 1925

When Fortune's celebrated its centenary in 1972, 75 year old William Fortune recalled how his grandfather, the founder, would have sold salt bloaters – there were no kippers in those days; kippering only started in the 1890s, indeed the salt cost more than the herrings at that time!

For much of the 20th century the family sent kippers through the post to all parts of Britain.

In 1991 there was concern that the European Commissioners would state that the traditional kipper smokehouses did not satisfy their new standards of

William Fortune

Kippers 'on tenterhooks' in the smokehouse

food production hygiene, but it has been agreed that smokehouses such as Fortune's should be exempt from such regulations.

Today Barry and Derek, who first became interested in kippering when they were young lads helping their uncle, have to rely on herrings imported from Norway and Iceland. These arrive in England by ferry to Redcar, having been frozen on the fishing boats. No longer do they post kippers to customers around the country, as previous generations did – but they are still kept busy serving locals and tourists alike at the shop counter in Henrietta Street – the only place you can buy Fortune's famous kippers.

FRIENDS PROVIDENT

Joseph Rowntree

Samuel Tuke

When Henry Brady, a master at Ackworth School near Pontefract, died in 1828 at the early age of 30, he left a wife and family who had to rely on the benevolence of the Quaker Meeting. The Society of Friends, or Quakers, were a strong community in Yorkshire, and Ackworth School was founded by some of their members in 1779; they were true to their cause.

Two friends and former scholars, Samuel Tuke and Joseph Rowntree, met at the annual gathering of past scholars in 1829. Samuel was about 45 and fifteen years older than Joseph, but it was Joseph who came forward with the idea of forming a mutual life assurance association. Both men had their own businesses in York; Samuel was in tea, Joseph was a grocer. Both were to serve on the York council, and both families were deeply involved in the Quaker movement. Samuel already had an involvement in the growing world of insurance, for from 1824 he had been a director of the Yorkshire Fire and Life Insurance Company.

However, it wasn't until the annual gathering held in June 1831 that a proposal was brought forward to establish a provident institution and mutual assurance society, to be called 'Friends' Provident Institution' – the idea was received with enthusiasm. A committee was appointed, with Samuel as chairman, to draw up a set of rules, form a table of rates, and to circulate the prospectus among Friends. They reported back within a month and their drafts received immediate approval.

Friends' School, Ackworth, 1841

The prospectus outlined the advantages of mutual life assurance, and also stated the types of business to be conducted – annuities payable from the age of 55, endowment or whole life policies, and children's deferred policies to be paid to the child at the ages of 14, 21 or 25. The Institution was to work under the protection of the Friendly Societies Acts, and was to bear 'the character of prudence and disinterestedness'. Additionally it was seen to be of great benefit for the Society of Friends to have their own life assurance association because the life expectancy of Quakers, living under their strict principles, was expected to be better than others, and therefore they would receive better terms than those offered elsewhere. Membership was to be open to all Friends throughout the land, but members were not to see it as a charitable association but as a way of uniting to help themselves.

The twenty leading Quakers who had drawn up the draft prospectus were appointed the first directors of the Institution at the Friends Quarterly Meeting, which was held in York in December 1831; however they received no fees for the first twenty years of the Institution's existence, believing that Quakers who undertook work for the community did so without reward. They appointed Benjamin Ecroyd, a conveyancer of 67-69 Market Street, Bradford, to be the secretary, initially at a salary of £200 per annum – he was to hold the appointment for the next 25 years, and during the early years he was the only member of staff, and his room over a confectioner's shop was the first home of the Friends' Provident Institution. John Hustler became the first treasurer, but did not receive a salary; he was a prominent Quaker and a member of one of the families involved in Bradford's worsted trade. With both officers living in Bradford it made good sense to establish the Institution there, especially as there was good communication with Leeds, York, and Hull where there were strong Quaker Meetings.

During the early part of 1832 the Committee gathered mortality information from Friends in other parts of the United Kingdom, obtaining details of births, deaths and causes of death during the years 1811 to 1831 from Clerks of the Quarterly Meetings. This provided the base from which tables of rates were drawn up by William Newman, the actuary of the Yorkshire Fire & Life Insurance Company, who also acted as the Friends' Provident actuary for its first eight years.

To provide the new institution with capital, a Guarantee Bond was drawn up in July 1832 and 45 prominent Quakers, including Samuel Tuke and Joseph Rowntree, subscribed a total of £10,700 to meet any liabilities which might be incurred during the early years. That first year no member died, but the following year one person, who was insured for £1,000, did.

The Friendly Societies Acts laid down certain regulations – a Society's funds had to be controlled by a treasurer and trustees, its rules had to be approved by a barrister and a magistrate, and the premium tables had to be certified by an actuary. However, there were certain benefits, one of them being that the Institution had freedom from stamp duty, and favourable terms for depositing their funds with the Commissioner for the Reduction of the National Debt.

In 1832 there were about 7,000 adult males in the Society of Friends, a substantial number of these being in the North of England. Through the regular Meetings of the Society of Friends a thousand copies of the prospectus were issued and part-time agents were appointed. These agents received commission for introducing new policyholders, but eighteen months after their appointment those who had produced no new business in the past six months were replaced.

The first policies were issued in 1832 on 'the

twenty-first day of the eleventh month', in line with the traditional Quaker practice of dating. Policy No 1 was taken out by Thomas Backhouse, one of the arbitrators, for the benefit of his daughter Mary at the age of 21. Of these first policies twelve were whole-life policies, most of the remainder being annuities.

The early proposal forms for whole-life policies required the proposer to confirm that he 'had never had asthma, fits or any disorder which tends to shorten life' … 'had not been subject to violent inflammatory attacks nor had at any time suffered spitting of blood'. Of the first 56 whole-life policies issued 37 proposers declared that they had smallpox and 19 had had cowpox, although surprisingly none had suffered from typhoid. Each proposal was referred to the directors and was individually rated.

When the first general meeting of the Institution was held at Ackworth School on 30th July 1834 it was announced that 54 policies had been written, bearing premiums of nearly £8,000 per annum, and a surplus of over £16,000 had been accumulated. Steady progress had been made, and this would continue despite serious typhoid and cholera epidemics, trade depressions and the Crimean War.

In London the two most successful agents were William Hargrave and Joseph Marsh – both were signatories of the Guarantee Bond and men of means. They became general agents and persuaded another group of Friends to form an institution which would admit non-Quakers as members – the rules of Friends' Provident determined that all policyholders had to be Quakers, or their very close relations or their partners. The National Provident Institution was formed in London in 1835, again being founded as a Friendly Society with rules and a Guarantee Bond similar to the Friends' Provident Institution. William Hargrave became its first chairman, but only lived for a further year; Joseph Marsh became

its first secretary and was its chief executive for 30 years – the Marsh family links were continued until his grandson, Robert H Marsh, ceased to be a director in 1941.

John Hustler died in 1841 and was succeeded as treasurer by Thomas Fowler, who held the

Market Street offices, Bradford, 1832-62

position for the next twenty years. By 1842 the committee's prediction that Quakers had a longer life expectancy was proving to be true, although this meant that annuity premiums had to be raised. Over the next two decades the Friends' Provident Institution grew significantly, the number of policies having risen to 5,709 by 1862, two-thirds of these being whole-life policies. It wasn't until 1846 that a director was designated chairman; until that time the minutes of the board meetings and annual reports were signed 'Chairman "pro tempore" '.

Following the passing of the Friendly Societies Discharge Act in 1854 Friends' Provident in effect became a mutual life assurance office, but it still retained its protection under the earlier Acts, and its funds were still controlled by its trustees. In 1852 the directors, reluctantly, agreed to be paid annual fees for their work, and then only sought £400 per annum. However, any director who was more than 15 minutes late for a meeting forfeited his fee, the time being set by the Post Office clock!

Benjamin Ecroyd and Samuel Tuke both died in 1857 – Samuel's contemporaries regarded him as the founder of Friends' Provident. This was a time when many insurance companies were being wound up, but the Friends had ensured theirs was built on firm foundations.

In 1862 the headquarters of the Institution were moved to 45 Darley Street, Bradford, remaining at that site until it was transferred to London in 1919. A network of agents was set up in association with the Monthly and Quarterly Meetings of the Society of Friends, who appointed them.

Until 1887 the annual general meetings were normally held at Ackworth School, and from the manuscript notes it is believed that there was little disagreement.

In 1870 the Friends' Provident Institution's funds exceeded £1 million for the first time; this rose to £2 million in 1889.

Over the years various attempts were made to widen the definition of members, but these were resisted; only in 1900 was it agreed to admit scholars and teachers at Friends' schools, and at other schools

Head Office, Darley Street, Bradford, 1862-1919

managed by Friends.

However, by the early 1900s it was increasingly realised that the size of the Quaker community had a very restricting influence on the future of the Society. In 1914 the Friends' Provident Institution finally became a corporate body and two years later it adopted as its seal an elaborate design incorporating the bust of William Penn and the motto 'Truth, Love, Peace, Plenty'.

However, another major difficulty faced the directors – no Quaker either in the new body or in the Friends' community was felt able to take over the leadership of the Friends' Provident. The post of general manager was therefore offered to Henry Tapscott, who whilst not a Quaker was married to one, attended their meetings, was a non-smoker, non-drinker, and a keen member of the Anti-Slavery and Aborigine Protection Society.

In 1918 Friends' Provident acquired the Century Insurance Company for £507,500. The Century was formed in Edinburgh in 1885 to provide professional and commercial men with income protection in times of sickness or accident. By this time it was well represented in most parts of the British Isles and had a good office structure to support its work – just what Friends' Provident needed. In September 1919 the head office of Friends' Provident moved to newly built offices at 42 Kingsway in London, and in 1920 the name of the new company became the Friends' Provident & Century Life Office, a name which remained until 1973.

When Henry Tapscott retired in 1945 he had transformed Friends' Provident from a denominational Society into a nationally-known and respected organisation. He was succeeded by a Scotsman, Douglas Pringle, who also was a man of energy and ability. In 1954 he had the vision to move those staff who did not need to be in London to a new headquarters in a less expensive venue – to Dorking in Surrey, where part of the Fraser Estate was bought; the new offices were opened in 1958.

Over succeeding years the Friends' Provident & Century Life Office saw changes which brought about overseas expansion for the life assurance business but difficulties for The Century's trading area, particularly with regard to fire losses and weather damage claims. On 1 January 1975 the Phoenix Assurance Company took over The Century and all its subsidiaries.

Another notable development that year was the passing of the Friends' Provident Life Office Act which removed the requirement for Quakers to have a majority on the board.

Stained glass window at Friends Provident's London office featuring the William Penn seal

However, the ethos which motivated those early Quakers, and was the reason for the foundation of Friends Provident, is still alive today. It is perhaps best demonstrated by their Stewardship Ethical Investment product range where investments are only placed following deliberations by a committee of reference which investigates the ethical, social and environmental issues relating to companies in which Friends Provident might wish to invest.

Similarly there is a continuity with the founding members in that Friends Provident aims to be a good corporate citizen, supporting the community in a variety of charitable, cultural, educational and recreational projects.

Today, Friends Provident manages £38 billion of assets on behalf of over 2 million customers.

Almost 170 years on one wonders what Samuel Tuke and Joseph Rowntree would think of the organisation to which they 'gave life'.

GIGGLESWICK SCHOOL

Giggleswick School is situated in the small Dales village of Giggleswick, on the edge of the North Yorkshire market town of Settle, and not many miles south of the Lake District. The school was built in 1512, but did not receive its Royal Charter from Edward VI until 1553, it then being endowed with estates taken from another chantry school in East Yorkshire.

The land around the ancient Giggleswick Church was vested in the Prior and Convent of Durham. In 1507 the Prior granted James Carr, the Chantry Priest and younger son of a local landowner, a lease for half an acre of land near to the churchyard at 12d per year, on condition that he enclosed it and built at his own cost 'one gramer scole'.

An account in the *Gentleman's Magazine* for October 1786 describes the building as being 'low, small and irregular; consisting of two stages, the lower for reading, the higher for writing, &c.'. There was also a small projecting building in which it says 'was once a tolerable collection of books, now dispersed'. This was the start of our story, of a school which for almost 500 years has served the local community and an ever wider patronage, one which today sees pupils coming from countries such as China, Germany, Russia, Spain and the United States of America.

When James Carr died, he founded and endowed with lands the Chantry of the Rood Screen at Giggleswick Church. It is presumed that the Chantry Priest also taught at the school. Henry VIII's Commissioners found Thomas Husteler, the incumbent of the Chantry, a man of 'sufficientlie sene in playsonge and gramer'; however both he and Henry VIII died the following year. Husteler bequeathed sufficient money to pay a schoolmaster for three years and also Thomas Iveson, who was 'usher', or second master. The Commissioners ordered the school to continue for a further three years and the monies appear to have been also sufficient for this.

The next year when Edward VI's Commissioners visited Giggleswick, Richard Carr, the nephew of James Carr, was incumbent of the Chantry. He was 32 years old, and taught at the 'grammer schole', as well as having a licence to preach.

John Nowell, the vicar of Giggleswick and a former chaplain to the king, and Henry Tennant, one of the king's chaplains, and others, refounded the school, and it was endowed by Charter – bearing the Great Seal – on 26 May 1553. This Charter, now a valuable historic document, is carefully preserved at the school. It granted to the eight Governors, one of whom was always the Vicar, the power to appoint the 'chief master and under-master of the school' and to make 'wholesome statutes for the government of the same'. Unfortunately we do not know who these first masters were; their names are lost in the mists of time.

Towards the end of that century new statutes and ordinances provided that the master would use only Latin, Greek and Hebrew to 'scholars of riper years'.

Reverend Josias Shute

At that time the school hours were from 6.30 to 11am and from 1 to 5pm! There was no room in the school for negligent and incapable scholars, and all the boys had to obey the two prepositors (prefects), who were appointed by the master to keep order and quietness in the school.

Early in the seventeenth century, in 1610, the school and the land upon which it was built was purchased by the Governors, and the deeds are preserved in the school's archives. During the headship of the Reverend Christopher Shute, from 1615 to 1619, the school flourished; he was the vicar of Giggleswick for 50 years and also chairman of the Governors! One of his sons, Josias Shute, who became chaplain to the East India Company, and later Archdeacon of Colchester, showed his affection for the school by providing in his will monies for the maintenance of a poor scholar from the school, at either of the Universities. During this period, fellowships and scholarships were established to enable pupils from the school to go forward to Christ's College, Cambridge, and as a result many boys from Giggleswick School continued their education at the University.

Those early buildings and the approved statutes appear to have carried the school forward to 1795 when new statutes were approved. A few years earlier a second school had been built during the reign of the long serving headmaster, William Paley, who held the post from 1744 to 1799. He had the satisfaction of seeing his son become Senior Wrangler (the best

graduate in Mathematics), at Christ College, Cambridge, and later an outstanding theological author; and also another of his pupils, Thomas Procter, become a sculptor and artist who exhibited at the Royal Academy.

As the nineteenth century opened, further new buildings were completed, including a house for the master, the funding for these coming from the increased income the governors gained by their enclosing of Walling Fen, and improvements to the farm which the school owned on the North Cave Estate. A new headmaster, the Rev Rowland Ingram of Ipswich, was appointed in 1800. Between them, Mr Paley and Mr Ingram were headmasters for exactly 100 years. The school had for a number of years employed an usher, but now an English assistant was also engaged to give instruction in writing, accounts, mathematics and other branches of learning.

In 1825 about 25 of the pupils were boys local to the parish of Giggleswick, with a further ten from families who had settled in the parish; the rest came from a distance and lodged in the usher's house or in other homes near the school.

The first school, 1512

There is a reference as early as 1516 of a schoolboy lodging in the village. The third school, built on the site of the original, was erected in 1851. Its architect was E G Paley, grandson of Archdeacon Paley – it provided ample accommodation but only for the next twenty years.

In 1866 the Charity Commissioners agreed to a proposal that the governors of the school be drawn from a wider geographical area, and among the new ones were Sir James P Kay-Shuttleworth, Bart., who became chairman, Walter Morrison, C S Roundell; all were well known in the West Riding of Yorkshire for their interest in educational matters. A direct descendant of Sir

The school and chapel

James is Lord Shuttleworth, the Lord Lieutenant of Lancashire, who was chairman of governors until 1997, and is still a governor of the school. In 1867 the governors obtained authority from the charity commissioners for the erection of the first of the Victorian buildings we see today,

John Keeling

these being designed by Paley & Austin, architects, of Lancaster. Appreciating the attractiveness of the area, the governors made extensive provision for extra boarders in 1869.

The passing of the Endowed Schools Act of the same year enabled the school to review its educational programme, and it decided to offer a liberal education of a 'modern' rather than a 'classical' type, for boys up to the age of 19. That year Rev George Style became headmaster; he served the school for many years and proved an outstanding incumbent of the post.

In the last quarter of the 19th century there was major expansion with new buildings and playing fields, and acquisition of land around the school. This brought a new school hall – a fine room 80 feet long by 30 feet wide – a new library with a valuable collection of books, science laboratories and lecture rooms, a drawing school, gymnasium, a covered playground and the first heated swimming pool at a school in the country. In 1887 Bankwell was leased to provide a boarding house for boys aged under 13.

Since 1875 the school had had its own services in the parish church, but in 1897 Walter Morrison made it known that he wished to build a school chapel to commemorate the Diamond

Archdeacon Paley

John Keeling

The chapel dome under construction (top), and (right and left) the interior early 1900s and today. Below: dome mosaic

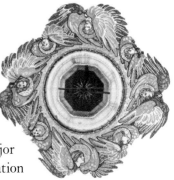

Jubilee of Queen Victoria. The architect was T G Jackson RA, and his drawings for the project were exhibited at the Royal Academy. Building work began in June of that year and in October the Duke of Devonshire laid the foundation stone; it took a further four years to complete. That month the drawings of the chapel were shown to Queen Victoria and Princess Beatrice at Balmoral, and they expressed their admiration of the design. It was a major architectural work, and the centenary celebration of the laying of its foundation stone was a major event in 1997.

In 1904, after 35 years dedicated service, Rev Style retired. When he arrived in Giggleswick he found a small grammar school; when he left, Giggleswick was home to a public school which had 200 boys on the roll and which was known and respected throughout the United Kingdom. During his time academic standards had risen to an all-time high, with many young men gaining exhibitions and scholarships to Oxford and Cambridge, as well as being accepted to military and naval training establishments.

Perhaps 1906 saw the start of what is now an important part of the life of Giggleswick School – service to the wider community. That year, in West Street, Leeds, a small house was opened, forming the Giggleswick Boys' Club. There on

David Hyde Photography

two evenings each week, during the winter months, some of the poorest boys of the district could spend time in warm comfortable surroundings playing games and reading; each summer term boys from the club also paid a visit to the school.

John Keeling

In 1912, the quater-centenary of the laying of the school's foundation stone was celebrated by raising a sum of £3,000 for the provision of entrance scholarships to the school, and the first were awarded in 1913.

1927 saw a total eclipse of the sun, and in Britain Giggleswick was on the line of totality. The Astronomer General declared this as the official site to observe the eclipse,

not least because it was readily accessible by train! There were cloudy conditions, but as the precise time arrived the sky cleared and a good view of the phenomenon was observed.

Over the next fifty years many major developments took place, including opening of the Catteral Hall preparatory school in 1935, the art department building in 1967, and Morrison House in 1968. In 1976 the school admitted girls to the VIth Form and in 1985 they were admitted throughout the school. New sports fields were opened by Michael Parkinson in 1994, and other important visitors have included Princess Diana and Humphrey Burton.

Each year there is a Sir Douglas Glover Memorial lecture; such celebrated personalities as Kate Adie and Chris Patten have been speakers in recent years. The school's Royal Marine detachment has taken part in a World Challenge Expedition to Bolivia, whilst other pupils have visited Sudan in conjunction with the Project Trust to work with chimpanzees.

Community service is encouraged and is a regular weekly activity – some pupils raise money for 'Friends of Chernobyl' while others help younger children with their reading in the village school.

Today Giggleswick School, with about 500 pupils, comprises three divisions – Mill House (pre-preparatory), Catteral Hall (preparatory), and the senior school. Style House has been recently refurbished at a cost of £620,000, which enables all sixth form pupils to have single study bedrooms, each equipped with wash basins and also computer network facilities. Other recent additions include a dining block and the Sharpe Library which was opened in January 2000 by a descendant of James Carr, founder of the original school.

It may be located in a very small Yorkshire village, but Giggleswick School's reputation is worldwide.

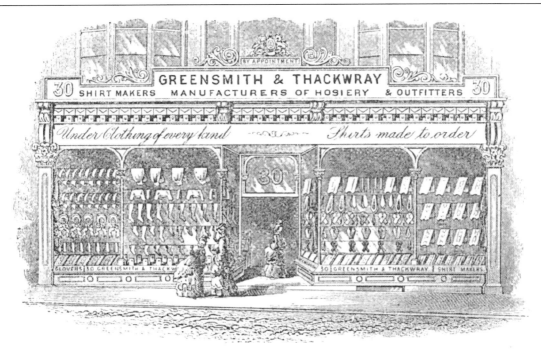

As with a number of firms started in the 18th century, it is now difficult to verify the original 'foundation date' of Greensmiths, as frequently this can relate to an earlier firm of a different name operating from the same address – this is the case in this instance. Although a date of 1789 is claimed, records do not exist to take us back to that time.

William Greensmith was born in 1792, the son of Thomas Greensmith of Watnall in North Derbyshire where it is thought that the family manufactured hosiery. Thomas was one of the first people to open his house to the early Methodist preachers, and as a result suffered much persecution. It was into that faith that William also grew up, and it had a major impact on the whole of his life, in business affairs, in the church, and in his service to the community.

The date of the opening of the shop known as Nottingham House in Regent Parade, Harrogate is not known, but on the front page of the first issue of *The Harrogate Herald*, published on 6 May 1847, is an advertisement which states that 'he has just opened his Hosiery and Lace Establishment'.

However, the wording suggests that he is a 'manufacturer of hosiery and lace at St Peter Gate, Nottingham'.

William Greensmith's daughter married Charles Thackwray, who came from Scarborough, and in 1845 he opened rented premises in the town, at 74 Newborough Street, which traded as Greensmith & Thackwray – that was the year the railway came to Scarborough. In 1856 they opened a shop, Thackwray & Greensmith at 1 Queen's Circus in Cheltenham, and the same year William Greensmith opened a shop in Edinburgh. Whilst the Cheltenham shop lasted for a mere 20 years the one in Edinburgh traded in the city for over 100 years, firstly at 101 George Street, and later at 110 Princes Street. William Greensmith's grandson, William Greensmith Downes, was responsible for its success, and the business became known as Greensmith Downes, and as early as 1880 was wholly owned by him.

At Scarborough Charles transferred to premises at 30 St Nicholas Street, the town's most superior shopping street, where they traded

as hosiers, glovers and outfitters, although for a while they traded at both addresses – it befitted a shop which had been granted a Royal Warrant; they were 'By Appointment' to the Duchess of Cambridge.

A further shop was opened in 1864; this time William chose Southport on the west coast, another better class seaside resort. The firm had various sites in London Street and Lord Street and various owners, only being in the ownership of the Greensmiths until about 1880. It opened an additional shop at 1 Montpellier Parade, Harrogate in 1867.

After a very full life William Greensmith died in May 1870, aged 77. The Harrogate newspapers gave large coverage, both in the form of an obituary but also the funeral sermon. From these reports we learn a lot of the founder of the business. He had been a dedicated family man, although his wife and some children had predeceased him; in the community he had been a member of the Harrogate Improvement Commissioners, but had also helped many individual people in ways he chose not to make public. In the

Methodist Church he had been a local preacher for over 45 years, as well as holding many other offices throughout his life. He laid the foundation stone of Bar Methodist Church in Harrogate, gave a plot of land for the building of a minister's house, and was generous in many other ways. One of the local papers described him 'as the most respected and honourable tradesman in the town'. Another wrote, 'There was no feigning with him, he was transparent as the light, delighting to do all things honestly and above board.'

After his death his son Henry, and Charles Thackwray, continued to open further shops with increasing speed, each one being managed by a member of the family. In 1872 one was opened in Bridlington, although it remained in business for less than twenty years; in about 1875 one was opened in Whitby, but again it was short-lived. A more successful venture was the Leeds branch, initially at 72 Boar Lane and then until its closure in 1929 at 29 Commercial Street. A further three shops were opened about this time, in Newcastle, Bradford and Sunderland, but none of then lasted longer than a decade.

However, only eight years after the death of his father, Henry also died. William had left less than £9,000; his son left almost £45,000, but these assets were dispersed widely, including the Scarborough shop to Charles; as a result the company was weakened.

From this time Charles masterminded the expansion of the company, each shop including the name Greensmith in its title. In 1879 an outlet on the front of the James Street Arcade was opened, not far from the present shop. The shops in Regent Parade and Montpellier Parade had both ceased to trade by about 1883, and with Charles Thackwray's death in 1891 the family ownership was all but over. In 1900 there were just two branches in Harrogate, the one in the James Street Arcade, and the other at 20 James Street, but in 1902 the name of Wm Greensmith

& Son appeared for the first time on the fascia of 8 James Street, and it still appears there today.

William Greensmith had held various positions of responsibility at the Harrogate Wesleyan Methodist Church, along with Charles H Barstow, in the years up to 1870. Probably from the time the company moved to 8 James Street and possibly until 1946 the Barstow family ran the business, turning it into a limited company in 1913.

Meanwhile, across in Scarborough, Greensmith & Thackwray continued to meet the needs of the 'upper class', being major stockists of Viyella and Jaeger, and Fownes gloves, who later merged with Dents. The business, which by now also included 29 St Nicholas Street, passed to a distant relative of the Greensmiths, Charles Dodsworth, who then sold it to Peter Neale who also had a similar business in Burlington Arcade in London.

Erwin Lobb who was head buyer of menswear at the large Sheffield department store, Cole Bros, came to Scarborough and became Peter Neale's partner. He was given responsibility for revitalising the Scarborough business; he modernised the premises, increased the range of ready-to-wear clothing, and introduced a hairdressing salon. Peter Neale's other business interests failed and Erwin Lobb became the sole owner of Greensmith & Thackwray.

Erwin's son Ken, still in his late teens, joined the business in 1938 and it was intended that he would learn all aspects of the trade, going round the various suppliers' factories and generally becoming familiar with the many materials, cuts and fittings. However, the outbreak of the Second World War curtailed such ideas as he was called to serve in the RAF.

After the war, now aged 25, he came back to the business, but by this time his father was in poor health and he had to quickly gain experience as best he could. In the 1950s Ken added an upper sales floor over No 29, taking over space previously used by Jaeger who had had an in-store shop. Ken Lobb became quite famous locally as a designer of ties with cricketing themes, having designed over 150 in his time. Sadly, with no son to take over the business, Greensmith & Thackwray closed in the 1990s, thus ending 150 years of serving the residents and visitors to this famous spa town.

In 1946 Edmund H Jackson, who had an outfitting business in York, bought a controlling interest in Wm Greensmith & Son in Harrogate, and he and his son E Peter Jackson set about restoring that company to its previous high reputation. However, in 1954 Peter Jackson had to take full responsibility for the business following the tragic death of his parents in a motor accident, only two months after he had been appointed managing director.

Since 1973 the shop in Harrogate has been a high quality men's outfitters, although it previously had a Ladies' Department. Peter Jackson has now been succeeded by his son, E Paul Jackson, but still the business supplies a wide range of quality products – worthy of the name of William Greensmith.

Established 1789

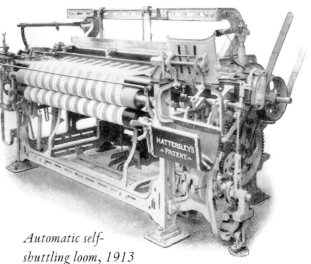

Automatic self-shuttling loom, 1913

Hattersley's has been part of Keighley's industrial enterprise for over two hundred years, indeed since Richard Hattersley founded his company in 1789. However, in those days it was a very different business from that of today for it produced screws, nuts and bolts!

The entry into the textile industry came in 1834 when George Hattersley, Richard's son, took over the running of the business and built the very first worsted power loom. Power looms were already used for weaving cotton, but hand looms were seen as the only satisfactory way of weaving high quality worsted cloth.

George's original power loom met a sad fate – it was smashed to pieces by a group of Luddites, at Nab Wood near Shipley, as it was being delivered to a customer in Bradford. However, a replacement was made and delivered safely and soon the company was making them full-time. Ironically they created jobs for the hand-loom weavers who had seen them as such a threat to their livelihood. The company changed its name to George Hattersley & Sons in 1835

Cloth measuring machine, 1912

and other new loom designs quickly followed.

At the Great Exhibition of 1862, held in London, Messrs Hattersley were awarded medals for their fancy looms, and it was really the effects of that event which gave the firm a new start to become a major force worldwide in the design and manufacture of looms. At that time places like Colne and Nelson were still small, but through the use of Hattersley machinery they rapidly became industrial centres catering for the new trends. Orders came so fast that delivery times sometimes stretched for two to three years.

Old buildings were pulled down and new ones built and re-equipped to cater for this demand. One incident regarding these buildings relates to an old joiners shop which recently-formed Primitive Methodists were readily allowed to use for a visit of a Methodist Home Missionary, Thomas Butty. In September 1821 John Laycock, a prominent Keighley Free-Church man, writes in his diary, "This day the Ranters

The OLDEST FIRM OF LOOM MAKERS *in the* WORLD

[Early Primitive Methodists] held a love feast in R Hattersley's warehouse, at the close of which the floor gave way, when a scene presented itself beyond description." Almost everyone fell through and one woman died and over 60 were injured.

In the 1860s Hattersley's did much trade with Germany, the trade in France still being quite small. In 1861 the company produced 829 looms, in 1862 1,220, and in 1863 manufactured 1,917 and four years later developed the heald machine, which became better known as the 'dobby' – this machine allowed looms to weave more intricate

patterns than previously. A great many improvements came from overlookers and users of their machinery.

Hattersley's made a lot of parts for machinery invented by Samuel Cunliffe Lister, the first Lord Masham, for his mills at Manningham in Bradford. There was a personal undertaking that they would not make a double plush loom under any circumstances, and although Hattersley's had many enquiries for such a machine Mr Hattersley declined, remembering his promise to Samuel Lister.

Another major development came in 1908 when the company developed the first narrow fabric loom – previously these narrow fabrics had to be woven on broad fabric looms, which was very inefficient. Even though the textile industry did not take to the new loom at first, the company bought Cabbage Mills, at Greengate in Keighley, and filled it with the new machines, producing webbings and tapes for a wide variety of uses – soon it had a full order book, and also a full one for the new looms!

Such was the demand for the tapes and webbings just before the First World War that they had to introduce round the clock working, even though they were employing 1,000 people.

After the First World War Hattersley's designed, built and sold thousands of Standard Looms throughout the world, specifically for the production of towels, carpets, cotton, plush silk fabrics and woollen worsted cloths, becoming the world's leading producer of looms for such materials. In the 1930s nearby Silsden became the centre of rayon manufacturing, and all the companies used the Hattersley Silk Loom for production purposes.

Top left: early Hattersley loom production line circa 1920. Left: present-day weaving plant

Over succeeding decades Hattersley's extended its range of textile machinery, and continued to supply many parts of the world. However, in the 1960s it, along with much of Britain's textile industry, experienced a serious decline in orders. For such a relatively small company to regain its position against much larger European ones would have involved financial investment far beyond realistic levels and so it had to refocus its aims. It attempted to diversify, but ceased trading in 1984.

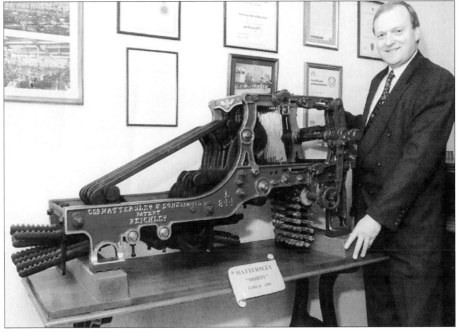

Managing director Anthony Woodyatt with a 'dobby'

In 1971 the Narrow Fabric production unit had become a separate division of George Hattersley, retaining the same directors, shareholders, and of course the Hattersley name and famous 'H' logo. With A C Robin Smith as managing director, and a keen and enthusiastic workforce, the continuant company went from strength to strength manufacturing narrow fabrics for both fashion and industrial applications, and became the world's leading producer of wicks for paraffin appliances – becoming sole supplier to Aladdin Industries and Valor International and many other companies.

Unfortunately Robin Smith had to retire in 1987 due to ill health. He was succeeded by Anthony Woodyatt, the general manager, who became managing director. Tony has been with Hattersley (Narrow Fabrics) Ltd since its inception in 1971, being particularly involved with sales and development.

The wick test and development lab

Today, over 200 years since Richard Hattersley founded his company, the name of Hattersley is still prominent among Keighley businesses. It is known worldwide, with its 12,000-plus webbing designs and probably the world's most comprehensive range of wicks for heaters and lamps, as well as transit strap harnesses for wagons, hot air balloons and husky dogs. The company looks forward to the future with enthusiasm and confidence.

Stocksbridge Works, 1848

According to Chinese legend the origin of the umbrella goes back to about 2000 BC. In that country, and in Japan, the umbrella was not just an item for keeping off rain, but indicated rank and status in society. Twenty-four umbrellas were carried before the Emperor of China, and no mandarin dared to carry the same number; the four-storied umbrella was reserved for the Imperial rank. Similarly in Japan the number of umbrellas, their colours and the material from which they were made, also denoted rank. In

Samuel Fox

India the titles of several of their princes made reference to the umbrella, titles such as 'Lord of the Twentyfour Sunshades' and 'Lord of the Umbrella'! In Siam the royal regalia included a seven-storied umbrella, whilst in Europe, during the Middle Ages, the three symbols of power of the Doge of Venice were the umbrella, throne, and sword.

Tradition has it that the umbrella came to England with the Normans in 1066. Early 18th century umbrellas were very heavy, having whalebone or cane ribs mounted on a long, one inch diameter stout stick, and were covered with a heavy cotton fabric, which was waterproofed by oiling or waxing. In such times there was little public transport and only a few buildings would have gutters or fallpipes, so water ran off roofs into the street, and onto pedestrians.

By 1787 Thomas Folgham of Cheapside in London was advertising 'a great assortment of his much approved pocket and portable umbrellas, which for lightness, elegance, and strength far exceed anything of the kind ever

By Royal Letters Patent.

THE NEW PATENT UMBRELLA FRAME,

OPTIMUS PARAGON,

MANUFACTURED ONLY BY THE SOLE LICENSEES,

SAMUEL FOX & COMPANY (LIMITED).

TRADE MARK  (OPTIMUS) ON EVERY FRAME.

OLD
RIBS AND STRETCHERS,
RUNNERS AND NOTCHES.

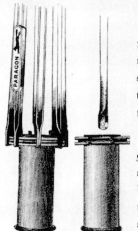

NEW
RIBS AND STRETCHERS,
RUNNERS AND NOTCHES.

The new improvements in these Frames are combined with two other Patents, and obtain in a remarkable degree such *increased strength*, with extreme neatness, as to make them the completest frames that have ever yet been produced.

The stretcher ends that are jointed to the runner, and the rib ends that are jointed to the top-notch, are formed into *hinge-like joints*, thereby considerably *increasing the strength and durability* of the Umbrella, and reducing its diameter when folded.

These improvements, besides imparting *greater strength, steadiness, and durability* to the above-named working parts than has ever before been accomplished, prevent also any possibility of their twisting, whilst their simplicity and smoothness allow of the usual *rosette* being dispensed with.

Samuel Fox & Company convinced that this Combination will be found of extreme value in Umbrella frames, beg to recommend it with Confidence to their friends.

STOCKSBRIDGE WORKS,
NEAR SHEFFIELD.

imported or manufactured in this Kingdom'.

'Imported' refers to umbrellas imported from France where they had achieved remarkable elegance, and were used as much as a sunshade as for protection from rain. Folding umbrellas, telescopic and walking stick ones, even the modern 'chubby' ones, all originate in this period. In the early 19th century ladies' umbrellas, covered with a fine pure silk fabric, weighed less than 1lb. From as early as 1851 frame-making, sewing and fitting covers was generally done in two separate industries.

A perfect Fox miniature with eight fluted ribs on a 2mm tube made for the Queen's Dolls' House at the Wembley Exhibition 1924

Samuel Fox was born at Bradwell in Derbyshire in 1815, and served an apprenticeship in the Rivelin Valley to become a wire drawer – one who draws metal out into a wire. In 1842 he took over a disused cotton mill and started to make pins for the textile industry, before commencing the manufacture of steel umbrella frames at Stocks Bridge Works, Deepcar, near Sheffield. He was a master craftsman, well known in the local fish-hook, needle and textile card making industries for his skill in producing fine quality wire, a skill he used in making fine umbrella ribs, wire stays for corsets and frames for crinolines.

At that time Deepcar was a wayside halt on the Manchester, Sheffield and Lincolnshire Rail-way, about one mile from the works, and Stocksbridge was but a little known village.

In 1847 Samuel Fox & Company introduced an 'Improved Steel Rib for Umbrellas and Parasols'. The first sales were recorded the following year and Fox's Solid Steel Ribs quickly established themselves – steel ribs had previously been produced in America but had not proved satisfactory. Fox's ribs were made of the best spring cast steel, which had been hardened and tempered, and where the joint, or git, lay flush with the back of the rib to avoid any projection which would have spoilt the line of the silk covering, and also have caused the covering to fray prematurely. The rib was not curved, as is normally the case today, this not being introduced for another 25 years. In 1851 the firm exhibited at the Great Exhibition in London.

Samuel Fox produced his first U section steel ribs in 1852, and further improvements were incorporated the following year; it was to become the standard for modern frames. After the Franco-Prussian War Fox's established a factory in Amiens, France, in direct opposition to Duchamp, its main competitor. The company only withdrew from France when the factory was destroyed during the First World War. Fox's adopted 'Paragon' as their trademark, which was later coupled with the figure of a running fox.

In 1873 Samuel Fox & Co advertised its patent curved ribs, which offered 'increased shelter from the weather and a gracefulness of shape'.

William Hoyland, the secretary at Stocksbridge Works, approached Mr Fox in 1875 with an idea that had been developed by Joseph Hayward, an engineer at the works (and the one who had invented Fox's Paragon rib). Whilst it had some advantages, Samuel Fox chose not to take it up and William Hoyland and Joseph

Hayward took out a patent in their joint names, registering the name of the frame as 'Flexus', and the company as William Hoyland & Company. They commenced business at Ecland Bridge Works, at Penistone.

Another development at Samuel Fox & Company, in 1885, was the invisible seam umbrella, where the whole of each seam was secured firmly within the rib (at no stage did they actually make the covers), and this was followed in 1902 by the 'Fox' Steel Tube.

Golf frame range

By 1934 the competition from continental manufacturers was causing serious concern; in Britain the multiplicity of sizes and types caused costs to be higher. Fox's decided to reduce its range of sizes and construct a new rib which embodied most of the special features from existing designs – the resultant patented 'beaded edge' rib proved such a success it became the company's sole design for the future.

However, outbreak of the Second World War brought normal production to an end for almost a decade, and then a new generation of nimble fingered girls had to be trained in the multi-skilled work.

Today another generation of skilled workers produces and assembles the frames. The 'Fox Cub' frames are made by taking hardened and tempered carbon

Sun umbrella frame

spring steel solid ribs and stretchers and fitting them to a springless wooden shaft – this gives a strong and wind resistant frame.

In 1987 William Hoyland and Co was acquired by the Readicut Group, and in 1988 Hoyland and Fox came together again. It has twice won the Queen's Award for Export Achievement, in 1986 and 1992, and in 1992 the Duke of Edinburgh presented the company with the Master Cutler Award.

For the 21st century Hoyland Fox will continue to make frames which will be used in the manufacture of sun, rain and fishing umbrellas. Eighty per cent of production is exported, the largest single market being France.

Following the recent growth in the demand for promotional umbrellas the company has invested heavily in computer aided design and other modern technology, and now produces 6 million umbrella frames a year. This has enabled Hoyland Fox to compete in worldwide markets, providing many extras on its products to give it the leading edge. Today the company slogan reads 'Hoyland Fox – Where quality is the name of the frame.'

LEEDS BRADFORD INTERNATIONAL AIRPORT

'Gentlemen interested in the advancement of the science of aviation' gathered in a room at the *Yorkshire Post* offices, then in Albion Street, in Leeds, in 1909, and decided to form the Yorkshire Light Aeroplane Club. By the end of the year they had 200 members and monthly meetings had been arranged where 'experienced aviators' would give lectures.

In May 1910 some Yorkshire flyers sought permission of Filey Urban District Council to use the beach for their aircraft, and this was granted. Among those involved in those early years were Mr J W F Tranmer and Robert Blackburn, later to be the founder of the Blackburn Aircraft Company; both came from Leeds. Very soon after they had gained permission, Mr Tranmer had a 25hp Bleriot

Leeds-Bradford's then new terminal in the mid-1960s

aircraft delivered to Filey Railway Station by the North Eastern Railway. A hangar was built on Flat Cliffs, between Primrose Valley and Hunmanby Gap, and a concrete ramp was provided to allow aircraft to be moved on and off the beach. However, Filey Council was not prepared to support the venture and gradually the flying stopped.

The same month that flying was agreed to in Filey, 'Aviation Trials' were held in Roundhay Park, Leeds. Year by year the Light Aeroplane club continued its activities, until 1924 when the

Members of 609 Squadron, Auxiliary Air Force, pictured with their biplanes at Yeadon aerodrome pre-1939

Air Ministry put forward a scheme to start flying clubs across the country. Through this the club got a grant and ordered two de Havilland Cirrus Moths which were delivered the following year. As the club had no airfield, the company's pilot landed the first plane in Roundhay Park where he was welcomed by the club's president, Lord Harewood. Eventually they negotiated to use an existing airfield at Sherburn-in-Elmet. One of the early club members was Mr N S Norway who was working on the R100 at Brough – he later became better known as Nevil Shute, the author.

It is said that it was Captain H V Worrall, an instructor with the Yorkshire

'Spirit of Yorkshire' – the first Jumbo jet to land at Leeds-Bradford

Aeroplane Club, who suggested the aerodrome at Yeadon as the site for a future municipal airport when neighbouring local authorities declared their intention to have an airport on the east side of the Pennines, not to be outdone by Manchester! During 1930 the land was acquired, and on 17 October 1931 the Leeds and Bradford Municipal Airport was opened. The Yorkshire Aeroplane Club moved from Sherburn to Yeadon to operate the airfield on behalf of the Joint Committee, but as it was literally a field it was soon realised that some levelling of the surface was needed. Yeadon had its first Royal visitor on 13 July 1931 when Prince George landed in a Gipsy Moth, piloted by Captain Worrall. It was also Captain Worrall who devised a scheme in 1932 whereby West Yorkshire bus drivers could be taught to fly for less than one shilling a week!

In 1932 the Airport Joint Committee bought Horsforth Common in order to extend the flying field, and in 1934 spent £6,000 on improvements. In March 1935 North Eastern Airways started a Newcastle-Yeadon-London air link, with a fare based on 6d a mile, and carried 600 passengers during their first month of operation. The same airline also started up a service to Edinburgh but due to heavy losses it was soon discontinued. About this time the Joint Committee went ahead with plans for its first short-range wireless station, and also planned an airfield lighting system. Various other routes were opened up during the 1930s but most were short-lived, the most popular being to Blackpool and the Isle of Man. An air link with York was also suggested in 1937.

As further expenditure was proposed, including £5,000 for a hangar and £20,000 for other works, criticism mounted about such enterprises being funded out of ratepayers' monies. But other changes were on the way as the probability of a Second World War loomed.

On 19 February 1936 No 609 (West Riding)

Squadron, Auxiliary Air Force, was formed at Yeadon, with Squadron leader Harold Peake as commanding officer. Initially they recruited locally, but lacked nothing in professionalism as a back-up to the Royal Air Force. However the Joint Committee was not happy with their presence and considered serving the Air Ministry notice to quit!

In December 1938 the Squadron was transferred to Fighter Command and Squadron Leader Geoffrey Ambler, later to become Air Vice Marshal, became commander. Soon night-flying exercises were commenced using Hind light bombers. During the Battle of Britain the Squadron had a remarkable record, achieving the second highest number of aircraft 'downed'.

With the outbreak of war, civilian flying ceased as the aerodrome was requisitioned by the Air Ministry.

It was towards the end of the 1930s that Roy Dobson, later Sir Roy, of A V Roe, told Captain Worrall that he had been asked by the Ministry of Aircraft Production to find a site in Yorkshire for a 'shadow factory' where bombers could be built, and to take a look at Yeadon and Doncaster. Captain Worrall is reputed to have said, 'Why bother going to Doncaster?', and he didn't.

People have long associated Yeadon with AVRO – A V Roe – aircraft. In August 1940 they opened their factory on what is now the Leeds Bradford Airport Industrial Estate. It was the biggest in Europe to be contained under one roof, and was fully camouflaged with its own imitation trees, hedges, animals, and even a duck pond; it also had concrete runways, taxiways, hangars and hutments. At this site, among many other items, 695 Lancaster aircraft were built.

After the Second World War the airport knew difficult times. In 1947 it was taken over by the Ministry of Civil Aviation and was operated by the West Riding Flying Club and Lancashire Aircraft Corporation, the latter running a number of holiday flights to Jersey and the Isle of Man, but in February 1953 all civil flying at the airport ceased; only a small RAF presence remained. However, in 1955, with the formation of Yeadon Aviation Ltd, which also ran a seasonal service to the Isle of Man, radio, approach and navigational aids, passenger accommodation and catering facilities were provided and the airport started to move forward once more. In May 1955 B K S Air Transport inaugurated an all-year-round scheduled service to Belfast, followed shortly afterwards by services to Jersey, Ostend, Southend, the Isle of Wight, Düsseldorf and Paris. In 1956 the airline brought London, Glasgow and Edinburgh services to the airport, but these, along with the Paris one, were withdrawn later the same year. Customs facilities were also introduced in 1956 and that summer the Lancashire Aircraft Corporation resumed their operations. That company was eventually absorbed by Silver City Airways, which added Brussels to its list of destinations.

In 1958 the Joint Committee had the runways resurfaced in anticipation that the airport would be handed back to them, and in 1959 the committee once again resumed full responsibility for its operation. Now that it knew the venture was safely in its hands, it provided new fire-fighting equipment, new crash and rescue vehicles, cathode ray direction-finding equipment, lighting, and a new aerial system for the non-directional beacon. Customs and passenger halls were provided, which included a public bar and restaurant; obsolete hangars were also dismantled and the facilities in the control tower were upgraded.

Aer Lingus, the first 'foreign' carrier, started to operate regular scheduled services through Leeds-Bradford, and in December 1960 this company operated an inaugural flight via Dublin and Shannon to New York – this gave the civic heads of Leeds and Bradford an introduction to

big jet travel. With the new links in place passengers could leave Yorkshire and arrive in New York during that same day; others went just for the duty free shopping at Shannon!

As a new decade opened, further developments took place – three-fifths of the huge wartime flight shed was demolished to provide more parking space on the apron, and once again the passenger hall was enlarged.

However, much larger initiatives were now needed if the airport was to retain its place among Britain's developing municipal airports – it needed a new 7,000ft runway, and all the facilities which went with it. Such a development would mean they could handle four-engined aircraft of all types and sizes. The Joint Committee was also looking at being able to deal with 2,000 passengers an hour; it really needed a new terminal building, with separate sections for incoming domestic and international passengers, and on the first floor administrative offices, catering facilities and a viewing terrace.

The Joint Airport Committee sought a grant for the work from the Ministry of Aviation, but as this was not forthcoming, decided to go it alone. Following a successful decision at a public inquiry, work commenced in July 1963 on a new runway which would be just over 5,000ft long, the successful tender being priced at £520,000; it was felt this line could be extended to 7,000ft at a later date without interfering too much with private properties. This involved creating an

The first-ever Concorde to land at LBA arrived on August 2, 1986

embankment at the south-eastern (Horsforth) end which took 300,000 cubic yards of rock and earth fill. It was equipped with approach and runway lights and at night pilots could see these lights from some 30 miles away.

During the 1970s and 80s there was much concern from local people about 24 hour flying. However, with the introduction of low-noise aircraft and soundproofing of some homes, these objections were overcome and a round the clock operation was achieved. In 1984 the runway was extended, as anticipated earlier, to its present length of 7,382ft, this including the bridging of the Bradford-Harrogate road.

Now came the opportunity for Jumbo jets to land at Leeds-Bradford Airport, the initial landing

Resident engineer David Camm with the tunnel excavation needed to carry the A658 under the extended runway in the early 1980s

Main departure concourse with built-in baggage screening equipment

being the result of much careful and secretive planning. Allen Rowley, the then Promotions and Publicity Manager with Yorkshire Post Newspapers, talked to officials at British Airways with the aim of running two 'round-trip' flights in a single day from Leeds-Bradford Airport taking in England, Ireland, Scotland and Wales. Just over 400 passengers were to travel on each flight and the Jumbo concerned would carry on each side of the nose the name *Spirit of Yorkshire*. It was agreed that the captain would be Yorkshire-born, and in the end all but one of the flight deck and cabin crew came from Yorkshire. The date was fixed for Sunday 4 November 1984, but then Gordon Dennison, the Airport Director, announced that Wardair, a Canadian company, was also intending to start regular direct Jumbo services into the airport – who would be first? (Some months earlier Allen had made a light hearted £5 wager with Gordon that he would be the first man to step from a Jumbo jet onto Yeadon's parking apron!)

The seats sold quickly and without any difficulty, and it was arranged that each passenger would receive a certificate signed by Captain Mike Webster. Allen went to Heathrow the day before the historic flight was due to take place and checked everything was in order – an appropriate crew, *Spirit of Yorkshire* on either side of the nose, and each crew member wearing a white rose! Soon they were airborne, flying to God's own county.

Sadly, over the radio Allen heard that a Canadian Wardair 747 was seeking permission to land at Leeds-Bradford. However, sportsman Gordon Dennison ensured that *Spirit of Yorkshire* landed first, and Captain Webster made sure that Allen was the first to put his feet on the tarmac. What a great day – whether or not Allen got his fiver I do not know, but he got a welcoming kiss, from a scantily clad kissogram girl Gordon had planted in the crowd of many thousands who had gathered to witness this momentous occasion!

Such developments as this have led to an acceleration in the growth, not only of passengers, but also of investment in facilities such as the greatly enlarged terminal building, a boon for those who travel and also for those relatives and friends who come to 'see others off'. Long-stay parking areas have also been increased and passengers can be transported from these to the terminal building by minibus.

The year 2000 marks the 70th anniversary of the Leeds and Bradford Corporations' acquisition of the site at Yeadon which has led to the creation of Yorkshire's leading airport: Leeds Bradford International. In 1999 1,451,201 passengers used the airport, against 1,398,363 in 1998. The regular daily flights from Leeds-Bradford to airports in Brussels, Holland (Schiphol) and Paris (Charles de Gaulle) offer connections with well over 150 on-going services to all parts of the world – Leeds-Bradford can truly say it is a doorway to the world.

MARKS & SPENCER

The exact details of the early life of Michael Marks are lost in the mists of time, but he was probably born around 1859 in what was then Russian Poland. From his earliest days he had what must have seemed like an uneasy future: his mother died while giving him life; and, being a Jew, as he grew up he was almost certainly going to suffer persecution, hardship and poverty.

However, when he was about 19 he left his native land and it is thought that he landed at Hartlepool, before moving south to Stockton-on-Tees and on to Leeds, where he had heard there was a large Jewish community. He was alone in a strange land, without any money that we know of; he didn't understand the English language, nor could he read or write – it was not a good start!

Amid all these difficulties was one saving piece of information; he had heard of a firm called Barran that was helpful to Jewish refugees. Trying to find the company he kept repeating the word 'Barran's' as he came to likely buildings. Isaac Dewhirst was confronted with this scene one

Michael Marks and Tom Spencer

morning as he stood outside his warehouse in Kirkgate, in Leeds city centre. Fortunately, with Isaac was his general manager Charlie Backhouse who understood a small amount of Yiddish, and gradually they gathered the young lad's sad story.

Isaac offered to lend Michael £5 – a lot of money in 1884 – which was gratefully welcomed, and he then used it to buy goods in Dewhirst's warehouse, which he then peddled in the villages around Leeds. He worked very hard although he had poor health, and he did very well; soon he had enough money to hire a pitch in Leeds open market. Initially his table would be only 6ft by 3ft, but with Dewhirst's warehouse being nearby he was able to return there frequently to restock. Soon Dewhirst's cashier, Tom Spencer, had developed a high regard for the young lad.

In the towns around Leeds, markets would be held on set days each week, and so itinerant market traders would move from one town to another with their various goods. Michael would have two tables on two days at Leeds market, but would also 'stand' at Castleford and Wakefield markets on other days. Soon he was not only looking to purchase goods at Dewhirst's but was also asking if they could help him staff the stall. With this agreement two girls worked for him while he attended other markets. When a covered market opened in Leeds, which traded on six days each week, he took a stall there. However, he was still conscious of his scant education and small knowledge of English, and therefore could easily identify with many of his customers who were either illiterate or had very little learning.

With only one trestle table in the new market he put a chalk line down the centre of the table – on one side of the line were goods marked at various prices, on the other a large poster, placed above the goods, read: 'Don't ask the price, it's a penny.' When he later moved to a larger permanent stall he put up a sign saying: 'M. Marks: the original Penny Bazaar.'

Over the next two years he opened penny bazaars in various parts of Yorkshire and Lancashire, and one even as far away as Cardiff. Pricing everything at 1d made mental arithmetic easy, and it is said he never kept any accounts so that wasn't a problem! However, it meant he had to search hard for goods which he could sell at that price, and still make a good profit. Frequently he purchased in large quantities to get a good profit margin, and one of his early successes was reels of cottons which he bought at 11s a gross and sold at 1d each.

His goods were divided into six categories: *Haberdashery* which included wool, hand-kerchieves, tapes, needles and hatpins; *Earthenware* – cups, saucers, plates, eggcups, pudding basins, teapots, tumblers, and ornaments; *Hardware* – hammers, chisels and other tools, nails, screws, locks, bolts, cooking tins, funnels and gadgets; *Household Goods* – soap, candles, wax tapers, cleaning powder, dusters, cloths, pegs, mousetraps and hangers; *Toys* – balls, soldiers, cannons, wooden carts, and children's books; and *Stationery* – notepaper, envelopes, postcards, pencils, rubbers, pens, pins, paintbrushes and music.

As the bazaars developed into a chain a centralised system of management and buying was developed, but assistants were appointed to take charge of the individual bazaars. Now Michael Marks concentrated on the purchase of the items for the stalls, sought new sites and supervised the assistants – quite a heavy workload.

In 1886 he married Hannah Cohen at the Belgrave Synagogue; it was the start of a most happy marriage which produced Simon Marks in 1888, and subsequently five daughters. As the trade developed in Lancashire, in the interests of family life they moved to live in Wigan, at that time a grim place known for its mine shafts and pit heads. Now he could expand into places such

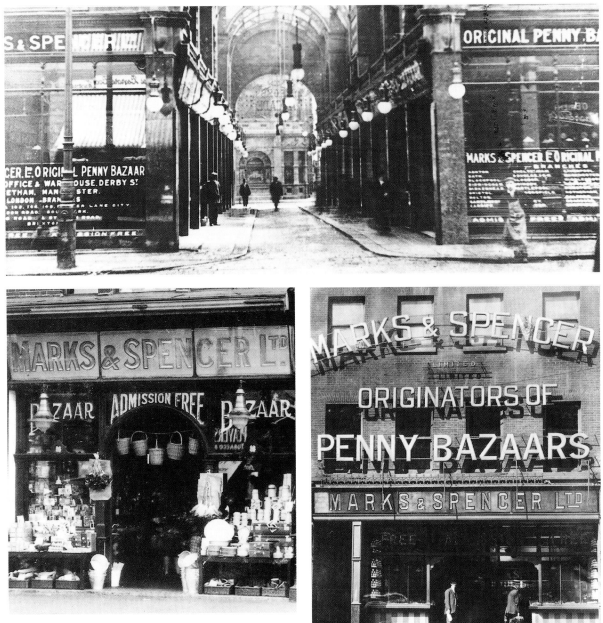

Early stores in Leeds at Cross Arcade (top) and Briggate (right) and in Tottenham, London (above)

as Warrington, Bolton, Birkenhead and the large city of Manchester.

As the enterprise continued to grow he sought a partner, and whilst Isaac Dewhirst declined the suggestion, it was he who recommended Tom Spencer.

Thomas Spencer was born in Skipton in 1851, and was therefore a few years older than Michael Marks. He was a big man in contrast to his rather smaller partner. His first wife had died while they were quite young, but in 1892 he married again. Agnes, a lively and intelligent woman, helped Michael with his English.

Tom was a good bookkeeper, and good with figures, but he also knew Dewhirst's suppliers and soon the new partnership was able to deal direct with manufacturers. He invested £300 in the business which represented his half share. Michael understood his working class customers and their problems, and sold them quality goods at prices they could afford. Simon Marks said some years later that he owed his social understanding to Michael Marks and not to Karl Marx! Although the two partners were different in many ways, not least that one was a Jew, the other a Gentile, most of all they liked and trusted each other, and on 28th September 1894 Marks & Spencer was formed.

Michael Marks concentrated on the bazaars while Thomas Spencer had responsibility for the management of the central office and warehouse, the receipt and onward transmission of the goods to the bazaars, and their simple accounting – each had clearly defined responsibilities and it has been said that this was one of the main reasons why they had no disagreements. Although their personal drawings rose as the years rolled on, they always left appreciable amounts for the future development of the business.

At the turn of the century covered markets were extremely popular places, not only for trading but also as places of entertainment – on Saturday evenings fire eaters and strong men provided amusement – and in some ways they were forerunners of our shopping malls. By the end of 1900 Marks & Spencer had 36 branches, 24 in market halls and 12 in shops, mostly in the north of England, but three of the shops were in London.

In 1897 the headquarters of the business was moved to a warehouse in Manchester, and two years later, on a site they leased in Derby Street, they built a modern warehouse, which had an electric lift and a dining hall where the staff could heat, and eat, their meals! Manchester was already a centre for international trade and culture, and the Marks family moved to live there and became involved in the larger Jewish community, which numbered around 30,000 people – there were men of vision, successful and wealthy businessmen, but people who saw the family as of great importance.

Marks & Spencer became a limited company in 1903, with a share capital of £30,000, almost all of it being shared equally between the two partners, who now became directors of the company. Thomas Spencer retired that year and died two years later – it was a major blow to the company, for it was growing quickly: from 36 branches in 1900 to 60 in 1907 – a national network was developing.

Michael Marks was a man of enterprise. In 1904 when the Leeds Estate Company opened the Cross Arcade in Boar Lane, the take-up of shops was slow; so seeing an opportunity, he took eight of them on a short lease and opened them as a Penny Bazaar. On the opening day he declared that they would not close until they had taken at least £100; by 4 o'clock they had reached their target and by closing time had taken £175! The presence of the Penny Bazaar helped establish the early success of the arcade, and Marks & Spencer realised its future lay in shops. Perhaps it was the extra burden, following the death of Thomas Spencer, which led to the death of Michael Marks in 1907, when he was only 48 years old. He left over £25,000.

The next few years were difficult ones as the various factions fought to control the business. Executors became shareholders, and William Chapman, representing the Spencer family, and Bernard Steel, representing the Marks family, joined the Board. Although both were now shareholders, Thomas Spencer junior, who had worked for the business for several years, was not inclined to take over the management, whilst Simon Marks, who was much younger,

lacked the experience to take on an effective role. Simon had been educated at Manchester Grammar School, and had studied abroad before joining the company. In 1909 Chapman and Steel proposed that the share capital should be increased to £100,000, to provide for further expansion. However, the trustees were not in a position to take up the new shares, and it was thought that the two Board members intended raising the capital themselves, thereby gaining control of the company. The shareholders, largely through the opposition of Simon Marks, refused to approve the move and the idea was defeated.

As Chapman had the support of the Spencer family, Simon Marks was placed in a weak position. Very gradually Simon started to acquire any shares which became available, as the voting power of the minority shareholders was now important — it was a slow and expensive business

and legal help had to be sought to resolve the situation. Israel Sieff and Alexander Isaacs became directors and this brought power to the Marks family, but with Chapman as chairman there were still major conflicts. After a confrontation in 1916, Simon Marks was appointed chairman, although only 28 years old, and Chapman and Thomas Spencer Jnr. resigned. In July 1917 Thomas Spencer Jnr. died and his shares were transferred to the Spencer Trust.

The growth of the company continued, and by 1914 it had 140 outlets, mostly shops, as well as warehouses in Birmingham and London. Working hours were long — 9am to 7pm on Monday to Friday, but on Saturday they stayed open until 10pm, or later if trade was good! This gave a minimum 63 hour working week, with a 10 minute cocoa break in the morning, an hour for lunch and a half hour break for tea in the afternoon.

Manageresses had a fortnight's holiday each year, and assistants one week.

The jobs offered security, were well paid for that type of work, and at Christmas the girls received a gift and the manageresses a bonus.

In May 1917, with the First World War still in progress, Simon Marks became eligible for military service and was posted to Preston. In his absence Israel Sieff became chairman, and directors' meetings were held in the Bull and Royal Hotel in Preston, so that Simon Marks might attend; later he was posted to London and resumed his role as chairman.

Israel Sieff was a few months younger than Simon Marks; they had been at school together, married each other's sisters, and had many interests in common, particularly Zionism. They both admired Chaim Weizmann, a great scientist and statesman, who led his people into Palestine and initiated the founding of the state of Israel. Simon Marks was seconded from the army to establish Weizmann's headquarters in London, and Israel Sieff was allowed by the company to work full-time on the cause and assist the Palestine Commission.

Wartime was not the time for expansion, and with difficulties in obtaining supplies they had to increase stock levels and therefore needed to negotiate a £75,000 overdraft. After the war they started to buy the freehold of a large number of their stores, and with textiles now becoming a major part of their sales, they created a new image.

In 1924 Simon Marks visited the United States for the first time. He particularly wanted to see how stores there matched up to the competition from Woolworth's as they were now impacting on their sales in this country.

However, he came back with a great deal more information than that, including new accounting machines and the realisation that every foot of counter must make its proper contribution to the payment of wages, rent and the general profitability of the store. Quick, reliable information was now seen as very important so that stock requirements could be determined – there was clearly a need for much rethinking and retraining.

Marks & Spencer became a public company in 1926, and the first Michael House was opened in London's Chiswell Street in 1928. In 1931 the company moved to premises in Baker Street, the present ones being built in 1958. In 1934 the nominal value of the company was over £3 million.

It was in the 1920s that Marks & Spencer started doing business with the Leicester based firm of Corah – in 1985 it bought £56 million of their products! Corah's factory was near St Margaret's Church in the city and sold its goods under the 'St Margaret' brand name. It was in November 1928 that Marks & Spencer decided that it also should have its own brand name for goods which had been specifically produced for it, and similarly chose 'St Michael' – partly because it 'canonised' Michael Marks; St Michael is also the guardian angel and patron of the Jewish people.

The now familiar green and gold fascia made its first appearance in 1924.

Over the years Marks & Spencer has developed close links with its suppliers, over 40 of them having links stretching almost 50 years, and Dewhirst's of course having been involved from the very first day!

In the 1930s many departments were closed to make way for quicker selling lines, as textiles continued to dominate sales. In 1933 the company started obtaining fully-fashioned stockings from Kunert in Czechoslovakia, and soon was placing orders for 25,000 dozen pairs a week, making it the biggest retailer of such goods in Britain, if not the world.

In 1935 Marks & Spencer opened its own

testing laboratory for textiles and in the following year a Merchandise Development Department – Chaim Weizmann had stressed to Simon Marks and Israel Sieff the importance of the quality control of its goods many years before. By this time foodstuffs accounted for about 11 per cent of turnover, and when it started importing oranges from Palestine, a separate fruit department was formed. Other introductions included sausages, cooked meats, bacon and cheese.

In 1939 they had 234 stores, giving a turnover of £23 million, but 16 of these were damaged during the Second World War, and after the war much rebuilding and modernisation were needed. It was also after the war, in the late 1950s, that St Michael became their exclusive brand name.

Today there are much stricter controls on the environment under which food products are produced and sold. Good stock control is imperative as all such goods have 'sell-by dates' on their packages. Textiles still play a very important part in the business, and while today many of these are man-made, and may be imported from various parts of the world, linen and cotton garments are once again becoming popular. Since the 1930s the company has had its own textile research department. The company has sought to contribute to the community by making major contributions to charitable causes, and by seconding staff to help with a wide range of important works.

For many years the name of Marks &

Spencer has been its best advertisement, because of its reputation for quality and service. As we enter a new millennium there are 289 stores in the UK, with a further 90 stores spread over France, Belgium, Holland,

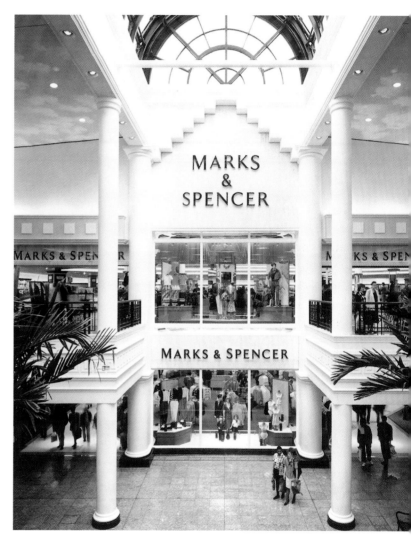

Meadowhall store, Sheffield

Spain, the United States and Canada, Japan and Hong Kong. Marks & Spencer also runs 91 franchises overseas, 191 Brooks Brothers subsidiaries in the United States, Hong Kong and Japan, and 22 Kings Supermarkets in the United States.

William Murdoch Morrison was certainly not born with a silver spoon in his mouth. He was born at Chickenley, Wakefield in 1875, and was adopted at the age of seven. When he left school he worked as an apprentice grocer in Bradford for 2s 6d a week, plus his keep! Later he went to work for a wholesale egg and butter merchant, before starting in the same type of business in John Street, Bradford in 1899. William was a teetotaller, but often had to go into pubs to get his boss out – a drinker of a lot of whisky – all this made a big impression on the young man.

Tragedy struck William when his wife Amelia died in 1919, shortly after childbirth, but in 1921 he married a second time, to Hilda Ryder who came from Hull. By this time Wm Morrison (Provisions) Ltd had become an established company, although now a retail concern. In those early days shops within markets were more like market stalls, being enclosed with curtains after closing time. Wm Morrison Ltd would be among such famous names as Redman's, Driver's and Maypole – all names familiar to Yorkshire housewives. Several of these businesses would also have small shops in rows of terrace houses, the owners often living behind and above the shop. By 1929 the firm had a mix of such outlets.

During the Depression the business fell on hard times and they had to start all over again, this time with stalls in Dewsbury and Bradford markets. However, Hilda Morrison was a supersaleswoman – she could 'pitch' to attract a crowd, her voice never let her down and she could do a hard sell to even the most disinterested potential customer!

William Morrison was 57 when Kenneth Duncan Morrison was born in 1931; he was the youngest of six surviving children, and the only boy. Ken can still remember that during the Second World War when many foods were rationed, the whole family joined together around the kitchen table to count the various little coupons that had been cut from ration books. During the war their main stall in Rawson Market was demolished by bombing; it was many years before it was rebuilt and in the meantime they opened a 720 sq ft store in James Street – it was Bradford's first self-service store, so small it had only three checkouts!

Ken started his education at Lorne Street Primary School, before going to Bradford Grammar School. When he left school he worked briefly for the family business in Bradford Market as a general sales assistant, but in late 1950 he joined the Army to do his National Service.

It was while he was serving in Germany his father became ill and his mother telephoned to say that he was not going to be able to return to work. Her question was, should she keep the business going until Ken was demobbed, or if he did not want to come back to the family firm, should she sell it? He had to quickly focus his thoughts, but he was soon able to tell her that he would take it on, and in 1952 he started a life in commerce. Soon he was joined in the venture by Ken Blundell, husband of his sister Joan, and Keith Naylor, husband of his sister Barbara.

William Morrison died in 1956.

When Rawson Market reopened in 1958 the firm took three adjoining shops, using one as a cheese bar, one as a bacon shop, and the other to sell canned goods. They were now keen to exploit the self-service concept, but they hadn't the money needed to pay the covenant required before they could rent a

William and Hilda Morrison in 1951

larger city centre shop.

However, in 1961 Ken Morrison noticed that the disused Victoria Cinema was for sale, and bought it for £1,100; it was about two miles from the city centre and they had to remove its sloping floor and balcony before they could convert it into a supermarket! Buying such a building meant that for the first time in his life Ken had to employ an architect and builders, indeed Geoffrey Haggas, the builder, said, 'We shall need a quantity surveyor.' Ken asked, 'What does he do?' But Ken Morrison learned quickly.

Fellow market traders thought they were

'barmy', especially to go into the suburbs. On those first Saturday mornings after they had opened, Ken had his worries as he saw busloads of people going into Bradford. Nevertheless it wasn't long before he saw his store busy with shoppers, and with the coming of the age of the car his success was assured. Shopping patterns were changing, and changing in Morrisons favour.

Shortly afterwards Geoffrey Haggas told Ken

about a site he was working on at Bolton Junction, on the other side of the city. Its owner was going bankrupt that night, and therefore if he wanted to buy it a decision must be made that day. Ken wasn't sure he wanted another site, but in the afternoon he took his little van and went and had a look. It was a cold, damp and misty day; there wasn't even a dog in sight, never mind a potential customer. In a time of crisis he believes in having a cup of tea to clear the mind – he had one, and bought the property! It cost £4,000 and Wm Airey's were appointed builders. Through this work he met Ron Curry who became Morrisons Property Director and played a large part in the company's future growth.

One day Ken Morrison was in the Bolton Junction store when he saw Jim Grundy there, whom he knew to be a director of Tesco, along with John Simpson, the owner of the local Woodroyd Laundry. John Simpson was obviously explaining to the Tesco's man the potential for the laundry site – but Tesco's didn't get near it, and it became a Morrisons supermarket!

Similarly, next to the famous Park Avenue cricket ground they converted a bowling alley into yet another store.

In November 1967 the company was listed on the stock exchange, and changed its name to Wm Morrison Supermarkets Ltd. A purpose-built head office, warehouse and factory complex was constructed at Girlington, not far from the site of the converted cinema, and named Hilmore House in memory of and with thankfulness for all the hard work of Hilda

Morrison in those early years.

Another innovation for the company was to include a petrol filling station in their development at Morley near Leeds; that was in 1975, about the time that they also adopted the term 'Lifestyle' to describe the growing trade in non-food products.

Expansion into Lancashire came with the purchase of the Whelan Discount Stores, providing outlets in such important towns as Preston, Bolton, St Helens and Chorley. Gradually a national network is developing with stores as far north as Carlisle and Newcastle, and as far south as Erith in Kent and Chingford in Essex. In 1999, the company's centenary year, William Morrison Supermarkets PLC opened its 100th store at Nelson in Lancashire.

As we enter the company's second century it now employs over 33,000 staff, many of whom are able to share in the profits of a business which still strives to meet Ken Morrison's original aims: outstanding value for money coupled with excellent service. Conscious of the disadvantages other people have to endure, the company and its staff each year work to support a specific charity – in 1999 they raised over £380,000 for the British Heart Foundation.

As the new millennium dawned Wm Morrison Supermarkets PLC was acclaimed Britain's top supermarket having been nominated 'Multiple Retailer of the Year' in the National Retail Industry Awards.

The Morrison family is still deeply involved in the business, and remembers with thanks the start and example provided by William and Hilda Morrison. Ken Morrison, now company chairman, received an Honorary degree from the University of Bradford in 1988, was awarded the CBE for services to retailing in 1990, and was knighted in the Millennium New Year's Honours List. Today the fourth generation of the family accepts the mantle and looks forward to the challenge and opportunities the future will surely bring.

Naylor Brothers
-RESTORATIONS-

Frank and Joyce Naylor were professional violinists, playing in the Hallé Orchestra; Frank was also a successful businessman being a director in F P Naylor Ltd of Castleford, a company involved in building exhibition stands, and also Shaw and Oliver, which supplied wicker baskets to Timothy, Whites & Taylor. Education was important to the Naylors and therefore their two boys went firstly to Far Headingley Preparatory School before progressing to Ghyll Royd School in Ilkley, and Rossall in Lancashire.

Alastair and David got on well as brothers, but David was more academic, and became an articled clerk in an accountant's office. Alastair, however, was good with his hands and had a mechanical bent. On leaving school he became an apprentice mechanical engineer at Greenwood & Batley in Armley, Leeds, studying for an HNC at night. While at Greenwood & Batley's he nearly lost his

Alastair Naylor (right) and brother David with the MGJ2 1932 which started the business in 1966

life when his overalls became trapped in some cogs, and he later moved upstairs to the safer environment of the drawing office.

In his spare time he took up playing a G banjo, joining a skiffle group which played in working men's clubs. He also became involved with Leeds amateur dramatics, and developed into a model railway fanatic. However, as he suffered from dermatitis he was advised to leave the engineering firm. Following this he had a spell selling encyclopaedias by direct sale, and proved to be quite good at it. Joyce, his mother, had a Morris 1000 car, but that was hardly sufficient to satisfy the needs of two lads in their late teens and it was agreed that David would buy a 1932 MG J2 he had seen for £30, if Alastair would help him do it up.

In the late 1950s-early 60s exhaust emissions were of little consequence – they fitted a copper exhaust which greatly impressed their friends! Some of these other young people also bought their own MGs, it was almost a cult thing, and on a Saturday morning they met at Schofields on the Headrow in Leeds and drank coffee.

Direct selling was not really Alastair's cup of tea, but for a change he joined Food Brokers, selling Uncle Ben's Rice, Matey Bubble Bath, hand lotion and other products. Just before his 21st birthday he went to Oxford where Sid James was launching a new product. Several friends went boating on the Thames, but Alastair fell and caught his throat on one of the mooring posts. At first it didn't seem too serious, but half-way up the M1 he collapsed and was rushed to the Brotherton Wing of Leeds General Infirmary where he stayed for six weeks. It permanently damaged his vocal chords, but it could have been much, much worse!

In 1964 he became his firm's star salesman – selling toilet rolls! However, he was still expected to give his manager advance notice of the calls he would be making. One day, following an article in the *Daily Mirror* about Alastair and David's interest in MGs, the manager did a check in York

Naylor's TF 1700 Prototype No 2 –
its first fully trimmed pristine
development vehicle

and Alastair was not where he should have been. He had gone looking for MG spares – he parted company with the firm and travelling.

By this time the pair already ran Airedale Garage and were getting more and more interested in this hobby of MG cars. But, not convinced they could make a 'job' out of it, Alastair got work selling second-hand cars; however, the firm closed down within three months. He never took another job.

Some American servicemen serving at Menwith Hill, near Harrogate, heard of the Naylor brothers and brought their MGs to them for restoration. David still had his original MG, and while he desperately wished to restore it, the pittance he received as an articled clerk made that impossible. Over the years they had accumulated quite a number of spare parts and decided to place an advertisement in *Motor Sport*, which suggested that they had an abundance of parts: they received over 300 replies. Over the years they had traded with Hoffman & Robinson, MG specialists in Bradford, but now they bought spares as cheaply as they could, selling them at a profit as they fulfilled their orders. Whilst Hoffman & Robinson's broke up old MGs, Naylor Brothers sought to preserve them. In the future, as cars from various marques

Austin Healey 100 restored on
behalf of the National Motor
Museum, Beaulieu

became similar to each other, older everyday cars became collectors' items.

Alastair and David's father died in the 1960s, his businesses having sadly perished before him. It was also a time of change at Airedale Garage, for David had to resign as a partner when this conflicted with his commitment as a chartered accountant. When Hoffman & Robinson's premises were closed, Alastair bought as many parts as he could afford, helped by some friends who invested in the company.

Richard Sutherland, well-known for his racing expertise, joined as a partner. Alastair entered motor racing by chance in 1968 when a friend went to America for a sabbatical, leaving his MG car with him, on the understanding that he could use it for hill climbs, but not circuit racing. In 1970 Alastair raced for the first time at Silverstone, starting on the back grid, but finishing third – he was petrified.

At that time he had a 4.2 Sunbeam Tiger – no MG yet, and later bought a Sunbeam Tiger Mk 2. When he acquired a 1947 MG TC he decided he would set the standard and upgrade the vehicle to concours d'élégance, even if it was to be used for racing; he also displayed it on their stand to promote Naylor Brothers.

He continually dealt in speciality cars, buying such as an MGB GT and an MGB GT V8 – but he had to curb his enthusiasm. As the business progressed he built up a Spares Division, buying as much stock as possible from the British Motor Corporation, as well as from other garages which had parts they regarded as obsolete or second hand bits.

As classic cars became collectors' items, shows were held in the Queens Hall in Leeds and British Leyland Historic Vehicles and British Motor Heritage Ltd was born. When the Association of

MG TC Midget, 1946, restored by Naylor Brothers and featured in the BBC TV series All Creatures Great and Small – it was 'owned' by vet Tristan Farnon who was played by actor Peter Davison

Heritage Approved Specialists was formed, Alastair was a director for 10 years.

As classic specialist cars became increasingly popular, but in short supply, the concept of building replica cars was conceived and the Naylor car was born – it was never supplied as a kit, only as a completed fully type-approved vehicle.

Allan Staniforth, the designer of the terrapin racing car, was appointed technical director. The project took up five years of Alastair's life. The car passed its various tests, including concrete barrier testing, at MIRA and was

Fred Scatley Photography

MG TC Midget 1947 pictured at Silverstone

1966 Radford Mini Cooper once owned by Beatle Ringo Starr. It was adapted to have a folding back seat to accommodate Ringo's drum kit.

launched at the 1984 International Motor Show. Due to the enormous financial requirements the project eventually ended in disappointment when Naylor Cars plc went into receivership. However, Alastair had completed five prototype vehicles and 100 production models, which were marketed through the Austin Rover network, including some to Japan – he still owns one of the prototypes.

The company was acquired by the Hutson Motor Company Ltd, and the new company used all the available Morris Ital power packs. At that time some people regarded the car as far superior to the Morgan, and whilst it was hoped to have used the MG marque, this in the end was not allowed. Today the various owners meet together as members of the Naylor Car Club.

Alastair Naylor, David Bishop and Tim Patchett still race MGs and won the MG Car Club championships twice in the last three years of the twentieth century – they won 15 awards in the Isle of Man in 1999! They are regular competitors in the Manx Classic five day event, the Historic Grand Prix at Montlhéry in Paris, at Spa Francorchamps in Belgium, on the Circuit des Remparts Angouleme in the South of France, and at Phoenix Park in Ireland.

Today, if a potential customer doesn't already own an MG, Naylor Brothers Restorations will find one at the lowest possible price and then restore it to its original condition, or with a colour scheme chosen by the client. However, most of the work they undertake is to cars already owned by the customer.

Famous customers have included Ringo Starr and Lord Montague of Beaulieu whilst cars have also been exported to such countries as Norway, Switzerland, Germany, Holland and the United States.

Joseph Needley was a farmer, and he married Sarah Winter at Owthorne, Withernsea in 1832. Their son George, also a farmer at Aldbrough, married Jane Duke in 1860 at Sculcoates.

George and Jane had four children, and the one at the centre of our story is the second child, Frederick Needley, who was the older of the two boys.

He was born at Arnold, a village about 8 miles north of Hull in 1864.

However, on all documents after 1865 the name becomes Needler, and now it is uncertain which is correct, although Needler is a fairly common name in the area.

In 1871 George and Jane and their four children were living at Argyle Street in the St John's Wood district of Hull. Sadly, the following year tragedy struck the family for George died of typhoid, aged only 37. Fortunately the family must have

Left: drawing of the original premises.
Above: Fred, Gertie and Percival Needler, 1907.
Below: Spring Bank 1905 – the horse-drawn van was used for local deliveries.
Right: jar packing circa 1910.

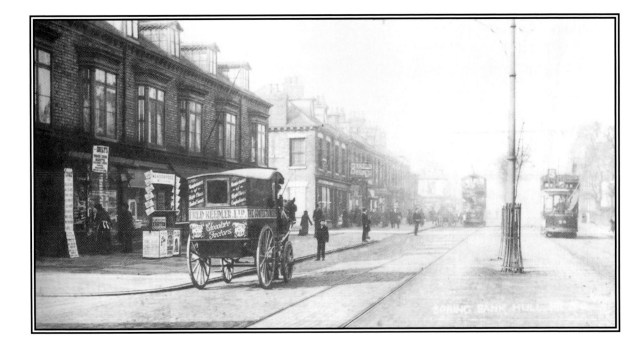

been able to support Jane and the children for they did not become destitute. Fred left school as soon as he could, because by 1878 he was working in a tea and coffee warehouse. It is likely his mother also took in washing, for in the 1881 census she is described as a laundress.

Fred must have been good at figures for when he was 18 he went to work for Edward Buckton, who had a small confectionery manufacturing business at the corner of Midland Street and Osborne Street, near the Paragon Railway Station. However, Mr Buckton's business got into financial difficulties and Fred was offered the equipment for £100 – it comprised two stoves, some slabs, rollers and other basic utensils needed

Ford AT 5624, new in 1920 and decorated for a prize

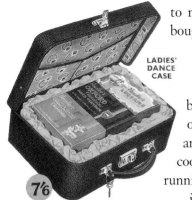

LADIES' DANCE CASE

7'6

to manufacture boiled sweets. His mother had this sum in her savings and bought them for her son. Fred took premises in Anne Street and started in his own business in 1886. In addition to himself Fred had a sugar boiler and a lad, and there was also a horse and cart on which deliveries were made.

At that time there were many small confectioners, each relying on a sugar boiler to provide the necessary skills; some would have a thermometer, others would just drop a small amount of the boiling into some cold water and watch to see if it set. The boiled sweets, in their various flavourings, were cooled on a slab which was kept at a low temperature by having cold water running through pipes underneath the table, and then either broken up or pulled into a rope, like seaside-rock, and then twisted on a further machine. The sweets weren't individually wrapped, but packed into large green glass returnable jars.

Soon, in addition to manufacturing, Fred also became a wholesaler and shortly had a flourishing business. He was helped by his younger sister, Lucy, but still he had to work very long hours. In 1890 he moved to larger premises in Brook Street, and in 1898 even bigger premises were acquired in Spring Street. One of his early innovations was to move away from using green glass jars,

Needler's

5'6

"RIPPLE" WATER SET

replacing them with clear glass ones which also had glass stoppers – being able to see the sweets clearly helped increase sales enormously, and in 1902 the firm was registered as Fred Needler Ltd.

The accounts for 1900 are still in existence and show that the firm's total turnover was £15,000, with a profit of £781. By then there was a staff of ten girls and 23 men, with a wage bill of £1,200. The price list ran to 17 pages and listed 38 lines of boiled sweets, 40 lines of toffees, 35 different health sweets, 14 pralines, and 15 labelled sticks of rock; additionally there were 65 boiled sweet products at a cheaper price, branded as Spring Sweets, making a total of over 200 different products – Fred Needler was no longer JUST a local sweetmaker!

Each line was made in very small batches, only against firm orders, with no products being held in stock. Fred also wholesaled products from Fry's, Cadbury's, Rowntree's, etc.

BUTTERED BRAZIL NUTS

In 1906, following further growth, land was bought in Sculcoates Lane on the outskirts of Hull, and a purpose built factory was created. When the building was complete it was equipped with the very latest machinery such as vacuum pans and plastic presses and the resulting sweets could then be produced in many different shapes and with a clarity never seen before.

From now on sales were established on a national basis, with agents and wholesalers ensuring a good spread throughout the country – sales also grew at a steady rate. Following the move to Sculcoates Lane, the company became Needlers Ltd, and gradually the wholesaling of other people's products ceased.

Fred Needler was a hard-working man with little time for involvement in politics or social issues, but he was devoted to the Stepney United Methodist Church where for many years he was a Sunday School teacher. He always gave a tenth of his income to charity, and also supported Tom Ferens of Reckitts, a founder of the University College and a fellow Methodist, by donating a residential hall to the University which is still known as Needler Hall. In 1898 Fred had married Gertrude Wood and they had one son, Arthur Percival, who was always known as Percival.

It is remarkable how so many confectionery or chocolate manufacturers in the United Kingdom came from either Quaker or Methodist origins. Fred showed his nonconformist sense of social responsibility in his annual bonus schemes for his workers, and the

provision of good staff facilities at the factory. However, in 1918 the Board turned down the idea of a pension scheme, as many of the workers were women and it was felt the men did not stay too long! – how things have changed. However, in 1922 a pension scheme was introduced – for men!

Back in 1912 the product range had grown to a staggering 576 lines, including 74 chocolate ones. As a result of this growth, a separate chocolate factory was built alongside the existing one in 1915. The production of Needlers pastilles began about the same time. At the end of the decade it is estimated that they were producing 650 tons of chocolate and 1,500 tons of sweets a year, and employing (including seasonal staff) about 1,700 people – it had already become one of Hull's largest employers. During this period all sweets were still sold unwrapped – it wasn't until the early twenties that wrapping started, and then each sweet had to be wrapped individually by hand – a most tedious task. Machine wrapping did not commence until 1928.

One of the company's 'problems' was that girls did not leave but stayed on into adulthood thereby qualifying for adult wages, although they had to leave when they married! One of its more joyful days was in 1926 when Edward, Prince of Wales visited the factory. That year the company also installed air conditioning

The eighth Coupon! — now for my FREE CARTON!

Miss Kathleen Singer, who won the "Yorkshire Evening News" and Scala Theatre Beauty Quest, says:—

"Here is the last coupon I need for my free carton! It is so delightful to think that just because I buy NEEDLER'S delicious Chocolates I can get a free Carton every time I have the coupons. I think it is a great idea."

FREE CARTON in exchange for 4 1-lb., 8 ½-lb. or 16 ¼-lb. coupons or mixed coupons of equal value. At all Confectioners.

Ask also for NEEDLER'S *Safety First* BRONCHIAL PASTILLES *In 3d. Packets or loose 1/- qtr.*

Needler's COUNTY CHOCOLATES

NEEDLER'S LTD., HULL, ENGLAND.

was clear that American employees worked about four hours a week longer than their British equivalent, but were also paid considerably more. The party came back realising that higher production was a key factor; it would be brought about by increased mechanisation. Sadly Fred Needler started to show signs that he was suffering from Parkinson's Disease, and he died in 1932 aged 67. His death brought many tributes in the local and regional press; one summed him up in these words: 'He was a faithful friend and a splendid Christian gentleman … success and honours had not injured his character. I never knew him to fail in honour or kindness, or in good sense, or in humour.'

As the uncertain economic situation hit the country in the Depression years, many people could no longer afford chocolate. Instead, they ate more boiled sweets; but these carried a lower profit margin. These were

and its own box making department.

However, things were not always easy, and growth did not come automatically – in 1926 profits started to fall, and by 1931 things had got even worse. The annual turnover had fallen to £328,000, only 40 per cent of that achieved in the early 1920s; the profit that year was only £5,100. In 1926 Fred Needler, his son Percival, and Clifford Thorpe the production director, visited the United States to compare production methods. They visited several large factories and noticed that there was much higher co-operation between employers, employees and the unions. It

Easter 1937 – such eggs were used for display then usually donated to a local hospital

difficult years for Percival to take over as managing director; yet whilst he found running the business a strain, he did succeed with the support of a good management team.

As the '30s ended and the country once again found itself at war, sweet rationing, and the rationing of essential ingredients, began. When sweet rationing ended, demand soared, each person eating 8oz of sweets and chocolates a week on average. In 1958, as sales and profits continued to grow, Needlers 'went public', although the family retained a controlling interest.

On the retirement of Percival Needler in 1970 he was succeeded as managing director by his son Raymond. By now the company had accumulated cash assets and some of these were used to buy Batger, a London based company who had the valuable toffee brand, Jersey Toffee, and also Chinese Figs. Batger Ltd had important contracts with Sainsbury's and other multiple grocers. Its production was moved to Hull.

Time moves on and Needlers had to move with it – they introduced pre-packed film bags of sweets, and also introduced better financial control. One of the benefits of the latter was that it disclosed that the chocolate trade was losing money, serious money, and that operation was closed in 1976. The resultant concentration on sugar confectionery gave record profits in 1977. A major investment programme, introducing a continuous plant system quickly followed, and new lines which had soft centres and carried the name 'Fruit Sensations' and 'Mint Sensations' proved a great success.

In the 1980s major export markets were opened up, particularly selling to the United States and the Middle East. Later in the decade in 1986, however, an offer was made for the company from Hillsdown Holdings as part of their

diversification, and this was accepted. In 1987 Raymond Needler retired, ending 100 years of family leadership in what had become one of Hull's major companies – Needlers, a name known throughout the whole of the United Kingdom.

Hillsdown sold Needlers to the Orkla Group, Norway's largest food and beverage group. The earlier 'Sensation' lines along with 'Butterscotch Sensations' were reintroduced in 1991 to be followed by Blackcurrant and Liquorice and Chocolate Lime flavours in 1992.

Recent research indicates that 50 per cent of children consume sweets every day, preferring gum, jelly or pastille type products, many of them being chosen for them by their parents. Needlers is now part of the Blue Bird Confectionery Group and is determined to hold and expand its share of this important market.

There was a Swan Inn in Low Harrogate as far back as 1700, where so long ago Jonathan Shutt received visitors at the 'sign of the Swan' and in adjacent cottages then known as Swan Lodgings.

Old Swan Hotel

As successive decades passed, members of the Shutt family transformed the Swan Inn into the gracious Swan Hotel. The cottages were replaced by a fine Georgian House in 1835 and the whole encompassed by four acres of beautiful gardens. Jonathan Shutt can rightly claim to be one of the founders of Harrogate's spa and tourist industry.

However, we need to see the development of the hotel in the context of the progress of the town, and here another Jonathan Shutt also played a notable part. This second Jonathan Shutt was born in 1779 which was before the appointment of the Improvement Commissioners in 1841. Acts of Parliament had been passed to protect the Stray and the Wells, the first of these – known as Tewit Well – having been discovered in 1587 by William Slingsby. He was greatly concerned about civic affairs and particularly so when he found that Joseph Thackwray, the owner of the Crown Hotel, was siphoning off water from the adjoining sulphur well to supply a suite of baths he had built in the hotel. He, along with four others, started a prosecution against Thackwray which started a series of moves which eventually concluded with the establishment of the Harrogate Improvement Commissioners. It was through their work that Harrogate saw many of the developments with which we are familiar today.

Isaac Thomas Shutt married the daughter of Thackwray's successor at the Crown Hotel. He was an architect as well as an hotelier and was responsible for the design of what was then the New Royal Pump Room, which was in sight of his hotel and near to the entrance to the Valley Gardens.

In 1878 the enlarged hotel was bought by the Harrogate Hydropathic Company who envisaged it becoming a replica of Dr Smedley's hydro at Matlock in Derbyshire. It became the Swan Hydro and by this time had 200 bedrooms with a dining room for 300 patients, a quiet room, winter gardens (conservatory) and extensive grounds.

At the end of the London season the 'elite' would retire to Harrogate in their carriages for 'The Cure'. In those days when many people regularly came to Harrogate for the benefit of the waters the Swan Hydro was frequently full with people who partook of a strict diet, medicinal bathing, exercise and massage as well as regularly

drinking the unpleasant-tasting and smelling waters. At this time the Hydro had its own resident doctor and also a resident clergyman. Once renewed, this class of visitor may well have gone on to enjoy their grouse shooting on the North Yorkshire Moors or continued their journey northwards to their ancestral estates in Northumberland and Scotland.

After the First World War and the Depression, Harrogate's role as a spa started to decline and the hydro suffered. But the years weren't without drama – in 1926 Agatha Christie, the famous author, who had been reported missing, was found to be staying at the hotel under the name of her husband's mistress, Mrs Theresa Neele, apparently having suffered a breakdown in health.

Just over twenty years ago a former head page boy, A R Morland, wrote down his memories of

principal trains and brought the guests back to the Swan, several of them probably crippled by arthritis or rheumatism.

He recalled how in the evenings everyone dressed for dinner, and following the boom of the loud gong, how the ladies in their lovely gowns, escorted by the gentlemen in dinner suits or evening jackets, would descend the grand staircase. Entertainment was provided each evening, and on Saturdays a grand dance was held in the ballroom, accompanied by a full orchestra.

During the Second World War the Hydro was requisitioned to provide accommodation for Government staff evacuated from London. By the time they left after the war, there were only four months in which to renovate the premises before it reopened as the Old Swan Hotel on 1st July 1948. It was immediately filled with a group

what life was like at the Hydro in 1928. He told us that whilst many took the three-week 'cure' at the Swan, others preferred the splendour of either the Royal Baths or the Royal Pump Room. At 7 o'clock in the morning he would set off to bring back bottles of Kissingen water from the Royal Baths and sulphur water from the Pump Room so that some of the residents could begin their treatment. On the way he passed Montpellier Gardens where already an orchestra would be playing. Each morning a partially disabled war veteran brought into the Hydro a large basket of fresh cut flowers which he sold as buttonholes to the guests. Daily the Hydro's minibus met the Pullman and all the other

of Soroptomists who came from all over the world to hold their international conference.

The hotel tried to make immediate contact with its pre-war patrons, offering a tariff which included bed and breakfast, luncheon, afternoon tea and dinner for 25s a day.

In later years it became the home of the International Toy Fair and played its part in providing support to the town's new found role as a conference centre. Today, as one of Harrogate's premier hotels, it offers those who come to the town on business or on holiday a restful stay near to the Valley Gardens and the town's fine shopping streets and conference facilities.

From  Redfearn
NATIONAL GLASS plc
to REXAM

When John Prince set up his glassworks in 1794 at Fishergate in York he chose an historic location, for it had in earlier days been part of the early Anglo Saxon settlement of Eororwic, and in the 13th century the site of St Andrews Gilbertine Priory.

John Prince, who was also a jeweller, was very successful in his new enterprise but when he died in 1820 the business died with him. Fifteen years passed before it was revived, when it was taken over by the York Flint Glass Company – the firm had been set up by Joseph Spence and some colleagues. Joseph was a chemist and as a result the company specialised in medical and pharmaceutical ware. An illustrated catalogue dated 1840 shows highly decorated glass jars and coloured enamel containers decorated in gilt – these would hold such herbal remedies as Peruvian bark, hartshorn, arrowroot and sarsaparilla.

Joseph was now joined by George Wilson, a man who has been described as having 'keen business habits and considerable scientific knowledge'; he became Sheriff of York in 1852 and the city's Lord Mayor in 1855.

The glass they produced was mainly sold to merchants and hawkers who came to the works to collect their orders, but later the firm employed its own travellers.

Although the York Glass Company continued throughout the 19th century the factory eventually closed. In 1919 a City of

London glass merchant, Charles Pratt, acquired the business but couldn't persuade the handblowers to adopt more modern methods and so transferred his business elsewhere.

However, in 1930 William Leslie Pratt, Charles's son, went to the York Glass Company to make the Fishergate factory more efficient, and its name was changed to the National Glass Works. Eventually the business was turned round, helped in many ways by the Second World War, when there was a switch from tin and steel packaging towards lighter-weight glass containers – their weight was reduced by 20 per cent and yet they lost none of their strength.

By the middle of the 19th century South Yorkshire, with its abundance of coal, basic raw materials, and good canal and rail links, had become a major glass manufacturing centre. Other firms such as Beatson and Clark, which had started in 1751, and Wood Brothers, formed in 1835, were also near by.

In 1862 Joshua and Samuel Redfearn bought the glassworks which had been built by John Wragg near to the site of Barnsley's old corn mill and adjacent to the canal. There the Redfearn brothers laid the foundations of a company that would survive the dramatic changes that the next century would bring, and then go on to become one of the world's leading glass manufacturing organisations.

Ben Redfearn, their brother, was apprenticed to the Aire and Calder Bottle Works, and it was through links with that company that they gained their early knowledge and experience of the art and craft of glass production.

Initially they employed about 200 workmen, who produced about 20 tons of glass a week. However, the company expanded and soon had four furnaces working, which fed 30 working holes, each manned by a team of five men. The company had its own barges to bring in materials and deliver the finished goods – they knew their business well and managed it very effectively. Each morning the day shift started work at 6am, working until 4.30pm; this was followed by the night shift which worked from 6pm through to 4.30am, the works closing each Saturday at 4.30am for the weekend.

Joshua died in 1897 and Samuel three years later. The estate was to be divided between Harry Redfearn, their nephew, and Harry Sykes Jessop and William James Asquith, but only on the proviso that the name 'Redfearn Brothers' was kept; Harry Jessop became chairman and William Asquith managing director. They continued to secure orders for the company's specialised and high quality containers, and also won export orders all over the world.

It was also their task to take the company from the age of hand blown glass, through a semi-automatic stage to full automation of the processes, where skilled bottle makers had to become flexible machine operators.

In 1910 the company became Redfearn Brothers Ltd, a private company. As modern production methods were introduced, the capacity of the furnaces had to be increased, and by the outbreak of the First World War 600 men were employed. When men were called away to serve their country, women joined the labour force as packers and checkers, but as a shortage of labour was still a problem the company increased its moves towards full automation. Quality was, of course, all important and improvements in glass colour were achieved by adding new chemicals in the batches of ingredients.

The first fully automatic machines were brought into use in 1925. When William died in 1926 he was succeeded as managing director by his son Harry and in 1935 Redfearn became a public company, employing 750 people. The machines were now producing 50 million bottles a year, or 27 a minute, these being made to every imaginable shape and size – this needed 20,000

ESTABLISHED 1862.

REDFEARN BROTHERS, LTD.

OLD MILL GLASS BOTTLE WORKS.

And at ALDHAM.
GLASS BOTTLE WORKS,
WOMBWELL.

BARNSLEY

Telegraphic Address :
Redfearns, Barnsley.
Nat. Telephone No. 96.

Manufacturers of

Machine-Made and Hand-Made

BOTTLES

FOR THE

Mineral Water & Brewing Trades

tons of Belgian sand and 7,000 tons of soda bicarbonate, whilst 14,000 tons of coal were used to heat the furnaces. Now furnaces and machines were working 24 hours a day, seven days a week, the men working six shifts and then resting for two days. Export production concentrated on beer and whisky bottles for the United States, while milk bottles were the major product for the home market.

After the war the existing site could not cope with the increased demand for glass containers, and it was decided to move production to a location at Monk Bretton on the canal, so deliveries of raw material could still use that form of transport; it was also near to a main railway line. However, it was still close enough to ensure little or no loss of skilled labour.

Milton Asquith, who had become managing director on the death of his brother in 1941, cut the first sod in 1946 and just over a year later the new plant became operational.

Both Redfearn brothers and the National Glass Works enjoyed prosperity over the next twenty years and in 1967 it was agreed they would merge forming Redfearn National Glass – the third largest glass packaging company in the United Kingdom. Things remained steady for almost another decade – in 1976 they employed 3,000 people and had record profits of £3 million – but in 1977 there were unwelcome takeover bids. These were successfully fought off, but in 1980 a worldwide recession, combined with growth in the use of the PET bottle, caused real problems and over a three year period almost 2,000 jobs had to be shed.

In 1985 the company appointed Arthur E Church as chief executive and it started the long climb back to profitability and reinvestment, coupled also with a move towards diversification. In 1987, to reflect its new portfolio it changed its name to Redfearn plc. In 1988 the company accepted an offer from PLM AB, a Swedish owned multinational.

Today PLM Redfearn, or as it became in 2000 Rexam Glass Barnsley, now being a sub-sidiary of Rexam PLC, is one of the largest glass packaging manufacturers in Europe, producing over one billion bottles and jars a year. Rexam PLC is one of the world's top ten consumer packaging groups, its global operations focusing on packaging for the beauty, healthcare, beverage and food industries, and employing 22,000 people in 30 countries.

ARTIST · REPORTER · CHEMIST   MARINE · FOREIGN SERVICE · AVIATION

WHAT SHALL I BE?

XXVI.—A VETERINARY SURGEON

VETERINARY surgery is one of the few professions in which the number of entries has shown a considerable decline in recent years. This decline is probably due to the belief that the expansion in motor traffic and similar changes have reduced the prospects of success in the profession. The belief is a mistaken one, however, for the decline in importance of the horse is being at least partially counteracted by the growing demand for the services of the veterinary surgeon in other direc-

When a boy who intends to become a veterinary surgeon leave school he may receive his professional education at one of fiv veterinary colleges. These are the Royal Veterinary College London ; the Royal (Dick) Veterinary College, Edinburgh ; th Veterinary School, University of Liverpool ; the Glasgow Veterin ary College ; and the Royal Veterinary College of Ireland, Dublin All students who attend these colleges must aim at obtaining th diplom of members' f the Royal College of Veterinary C

SINCLAIR AND WIGHT

Donald Sinclair was born in Harrogate in 1911. His parents lived in Green Lane, his father coming from Orkney in the north of Scotland, his mother from Altrincham in Cheshire. Donald was the middle child of three – he had an elder sister, Elsa, and a younger brother Brian. At school he had always been good at mathematics and had anticipated becoming an accountant. However, he also had a

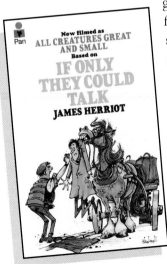

Pan
Now filmed as
ALL CREATURES GREAT AND SMALL
Based on
IF ONLY THEY COULD TALK
JAMES HERRIOT

great love of horses and a friend of the family, who shared that passion, suggested that a life as a vet would bring him much nearer to those and other animals than if he was shut away in an office.

It was advice he took, and never regretted. He trained at the Royal Dick Veterinary College in Edinburgh, qualifying in 1933, but then staying on for a year to complete his training. On leaving college he went to work for the Ministry of Agriculture in Settle, working on sheep scab, mainly checking sheep flocks in the area.

This, however, did not really fulfil his needs, and when he saw a veterinary practice in Thirsk advertised for sale he decided to move there. The practice was very run down and needed much hard work to build it up again. Soon, however, he had established a subsidiary practice in Leyburn, in Wensley-dale, and he carried out a lot of work for the Ministry of Agri-culture checking cows for signs of tuber-culosis.

As the work

Pan
Now filmed as
ALL CREATURES GREAT AND SMALL
Based on
IT SHOULDN'T HAPPEN TO A VET
JAMES HERRIOT

expanded, it became apparent that an extra pair of hands was needed and so an advertisement was placed in the *Veterinary Record*.

Among the applicants was one James Alfred Wight.

James Alfred Wight had been born in Sunderland in 1916, the only child of James (Jim) Henry Wight and his wife Hannah. After their wedding, Jim and Hannah had moved to live in Glasgow, but she returned to have their baby in her family home.

Jim was a ship plater and worked in the booming Sunderland shipyards where he enjoyed his work. But in 1914, shortly before their wedding, he moved to similar work in Glasgow. Both Jim and Hannah loved music and saw Glasgow as a cultural city where they could develop those

Where it all began for Alf Wight, alias James Herriot (above) – an article in the Meccano magazine (left).

interests. Young Alf would also develop a love of Glasgow and come to regard himself as a true 'Glaswegian'.

Alf grew up in the family home in Yoker, a suburb of the city; it was a ground-floor flat in a rather better than average tenement in Yoker Road (it later became Dumbarton Road) – this was not the slum type of property so often associated with tenement buildings. Nearby were the Kilpatrick Hills, farmlands and green fields, and in the further distance the Campsie Fells.

His was a good home, a church going home, where his father spent hours playing his grand

piano after a day's work, and where his mother did dressmaking as a business.

His education began at Yoker Primary School, followed by attendance at Hillhead High School, one of Glasgow's foremost fee-paying schools. There was much competition for places at the school, many of the children coming from much more affluent homes than Alf's. At this time life on the docks was hard and his father had been made redundant, so they had to rely on Jim's piano playing at the cinemas and theatres, as well as what he could make from doing joinery work. However the money that Alf's mother brought in with her dressmaking and piano lessons was a great help in paying his school fees. It was at Hillhead that he acquired the attributes which would be hallmarks of his character later in life – his great enthusiasm for everything he did, his ambition to succeed, and his love of music, sport and literature. Alf realised how much his education meant to his parents and he was ever grateful for the sacrifices they made.

Alf Wight knew disappointment and frustration during those schooldays for he suffered from, and nearly died from, diptheria. He was also troubled with boils and abesses. However, he did not let this get him down, and as he recovered he renewed his commitment to succeed. School holidays with the family in Sunderland only served to

*Autumn term report for
Alf's first year at veterinary college*

confirm his devotion to Sunderland Football Club – a love that was paramount throughout the whole of his life.

1928 was an important year in the life of our future vet – as a reward for gaining entry to Hillhead School his parents gave him an Irish Setter puppy, which he called Don. They walked miles together, never to be separated. Other important events included seeing a careers article in *The Meccano Magazine* by the President of the Royal College of Veterinary Surgeons, and a visit to Hillhead School by the principal of the Glasgow Veterinary College. Alf took up the principal's offer to visit the college where he was told he was unlikely to grow rich as a veterinary surgeon, but that he would have a varied, active and rewarding life. He had found his life's goal – he would never regret the decision he made at that time; being a vet would truly give him fulfilment and rewards beyond measure; but he would also know the difficulties of little money and other frustrations.

James Alfred Wight entered Glasgow

Veterinary College in 1933, supported by an £18 Carnegie Bursary, a £10 Glasgow Education Authority grant and once again the generous and enthusiastic support of his parents – for yet another six years they would be there, supporting, guiding, and encouraging. Others may have taken a lax approach to their studies, but Alf knew how much he owed to his parents and he was determined not to let them down. However, once again serious illness affected him and his grades – it was a health problem that would afflict him for the rest of his life.

On 14 December 1939 Alfred Wight qualified from the College and became a full member of the Royal College of Veterinary Surgeons.

Alf was very fortunate for he had a job waiting for him in Sunderland where he would learn much about the practice of veterinary science – particularly with domestic pets. He was paid £3.3s a week and for that had to work almost every night with only an occasional Sunday afternoon off. Many of his friends had to offer their services for no financial reward. However, after six months it was time to move on. He applied for a job at Guisborough but was turned down. He then saw a post advertised at Thirsk – where was that he wondered? The details told him that the principal veterinary surgeon was D V Sinclair and that the work was mainly agricultural. He applied, and in June 1940 found himself travelling to Thirsk for an interview.

When he knocked on the door of 23 Kirkgate expecting to meet Donald Sinclair, he discovered he was not at home for the vet had forgotten he had made the appointment! Alf waited in the garden, fell asleep and awoke to find his future boss standing in front of him. However, he was soon very much awake as he was whisked around country lanes at great speed as Donald showed him some of the farms the practice served. After an even speedier run round the surgery Alf was informed the job was his! On 18 July 1940 he moved into the upstairs rooms at 23 Kirkgate, Thirsk – his life's adventure was just about to begin, and with a very different ending to what he could ever have dreamed on that summer's day. However, he would be working the practice single-handed as Donald and his other assistant were about to join the Royal Air Force.

Alf threw himself into his work; he was out long hours and then there were the books to keep on his return. The winters were hard with much snow and his little car struggled on many, many occasions. Nevertheless, he fell in love with the countryside of the Yorkshire Dales and the North York Moors and came to respect the farmers. He learned much as each new day brought fresh challenges and experiences – he also had to learn a new language, that of the Dales folk! All the time incidents and anecdotes were being accumulated in his memory – they would come out fresh many years later. At that time most of the money came from TB testing cattle, and quite a bit of time was spent in the ancillary practice at Leyburn, which eventually became Bingham, Sinclair and Wight – Frank Bingham being a larger than life vet who was later to feature prominently in Alf's writings.

When Donald returned from the Air Force, quicker than either he or Alf had expected, he sent the young vet to Glasgow to pick up a car Donald

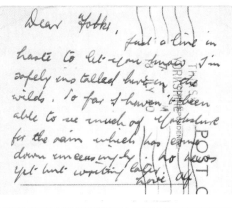

had bought and also to pick up Brian, his boss's younger brother, who was also training to be a vet.

Brian Sinclair was quite different from Donald. The pair enjoyed a wonderful love-hate relationship and Alf enjoyed every moment of it; memories are made of such things. Brian regularly failed his exams, and Donald, who was funding his training, regularly exploded in disgust.

It was through Brian that Alf met Joan Danbury at a dance at nearby Sandhutton – she would become Alf's wife and would also figure prominently in his later writings. They were married on 5 November 1941 at the parish church in Thirsk at 8 o'clock in the morning – the only people present besides the wedding pair were the best man, Donald Sinclair, Joan's employer and the Canon. Their honeymoon was spent at the Wheatsheaf Inn in Carperby in Wensleydale – two days being spent TB testing cows on hill farms in Wensleydale! As farmers' wives discovered that the two were on honeymoon they gave them royal treatment with farmhouse meals and gifts of ham, eggs and cheese to take back with them.

Soon they had made their home in the upper-reaches of No. 23. Joan was a great support to Alf, theirs was a romance that would last until the day Alf died; they would also

Postcard home shortly after arrival in Thirsk

become devoted parents and grandparents. However, one year after they were married Alf was called up and also joined the RAF – what sadness was theirs at parting – but a year later he was back home, having been declared medically unfit. While he was away Donald, a widower, had remarried and the couple had moved into the headquarters of the practice; Joan and Alf now had to live with Joan's parents, but they were very close and it worked out very satisfactorily.

In January 1944 Alf sought to become a full partner but was refused. About this time he considered other practices and agreed to go to Stafford. He even fixed up his replacement, but then his new job fell through. Fortuitously the new vet decided the practice in Thirsk was not for him and Alf was able to return to his previous position. It wasn't until 1949 that Alf finally became a full partner.

In 1945 Donald and Audrey Sinclair moved out of 23 Kirkgate and the Wights moved back, along with Joan's mother, who was now a widow, and who would live with them for the next 30 years. They already had young Jim, and soon there would be Rosie – the family would be complete. His other great love also never left him, his devotion to Sunderland Football Club. Whenever he had the chance he went north to watch the red and white stripes – his idols!

It wasn't until 1953 that the Wights got their own home, in Topcliffe Road, Thirsk. As the practice became busier assistants were employed and Alf at last found some financial security, although even a decade later he had little in the bank, but at least he had some relief from the seven days, and nights, a week. Two of these young assistants, John Crooks and Brian Nettleton, would become life long friends and an inspiration to him in other ways. During the 1950s the practice also started to change, the amount of small animal work increasing dramatically, and again this increased the number

of 'characters' with whom Alf came into contact.

In the late 1950s Alf Wight had bought some books on writing, for writing a book had been on his mind for over 20 years. At first he just could not get the stories right – he wrote about seven or eight and sent them to selected magazines, but without any success. Frequently he would tell Joan of incidents that had occurred on his rounds and say, "It would be a good story for the book". She regaled him with how he had been going to write a book for over 20 years and how men of almost 50 don't start writing books!

Her remarks hit hard and in the autumn of 1965 he started diligently, writing about the subject he knew best – the life of a vet. It wasn't finished until the spring of 1967, but he was pleased with it and felt it could be enjoyed by people of all ages. Joan remembered how Michael Joseph Ltd had published the *Doctor in the House* books, so why not send his manuscript there – at least the books had a similar approach, medical hilarity! However, a friend had had some work published by Collins, and so in the end it was posted to them. He had written it as a novel, suggesting the title *The Art and the Science*, but at Collins Julia Wadham suggested that he turn it into an autobiography for it was so obviously drawn from real life – it was the best advice he could have received!

It was at this time that young Jim Wight came back to work in the Thirsk practice, having trained at his father's college in Glasgow. He was able to relieve his father of some of the night duties and give him more time to rewrite his book. He did his typing in the sitting room, while the rest of the family watched television, and by the summer of 1968 the book was ready to be resubmitted to the publishers; this time with the suggested title *If Only They Could Talk*. However, once again, after many delays, it was rejected. It was the final blow; he would once again put all his efforts into being a vet – he was no good as a writer!

Alf with, clockwise from above: Donald Sinclair 'Siegfried' left and Brian Sinclair 'Tristan' right; veterinary son Jimmy; daughter Rosie in the Lakes.

Outside the Kirkgate surgery

Quite surprisingly, one day in the spring of 1969, Joan suggested that he should send the manuscript to Michael Joseph as they had originally intended. So he once again took it from the drawer, but remembered he had once read a book which recommended that would-be authors should approach an agent. And this was what he did – one Jean LeRoy. Within a week his hopes were once again raised. Her company also felt Michael Joseph was an appropriate publisher and a further letter, dated 18 June 1969, told him the book would definitely be published. It was one of the greatest moments of Alf's life. As a veterinary surgeon he could not write under his own name as it might be construed as advertising, so he had to search for a nom-de-plume. While watching football on television on 11 February 1969 he noted that the Birmingham goalkeeper was called Jim Herriot – he liked the name – however, they were not to meet for another 19 years.

For his first book he received an advance of £200 on signing the contract, and a further £200 when the book was published. He also received 10 per cent royalties for the first 2,000 copies, rising to $17^{1}/_{2}$ per cent should it become a bestseller. In November his agent sold the serial rights to the London *Evening Standard* – they were to pay £36,710. Alf could hardly believe it. When

If Only They Could Talk was published in April 1970 3,000 copies were printed, and a further 1,000 came later that year. In those first weeks Alf knew the disappointment of seeing few, if any, copies of his book on the bookshop shelves – things would be very different later. The characters of James Herriot (Alf Wight), Helen (Joan), Siegfried (Donald Sinclair), Tristan (Brian Sinclair) and later Calum (Brian Nettleton) had come to life in the various stories, along with many other local people.

His second book *It Shouldn't Happen to a Vet* was published in January 1972, again being serialised in the London *Evening Standard* prior to publication, this giving very good publicity. As other books followed the publicity increased as did the size of the initial printing, but they were still minute compared with what would come in later years. From 1973 onwards his books quickly progressed to top of the bestseller lists. When his fourth book *Vet in Harness* was published in 1974 the publishers printed 20,000 copies; and when *Vets Might Fly* was published in 1976 that figure rose to 60,000! Paperback copies, even more prolific in numbers, soon followed and James Herriot was becoming known far beyond the shores of Britain. The books were translated into many languages and Alf, alias James Herriot, became known as the 'World's Most Famous Vet'. Even the practice waiting room became invaded by his fans. One day he told young Jim, who thought it was going to be a busy surgery, that the crowd consisted of two hamsters, one Yorkshire Terrier and 45 Americans! But even in those heady days the practice and his work of alleviating pain in animals was still very important to him and he would always find time to discuss a tricky case.

In the spring of 1975 a film called *All Creatures Great and Small* was released in Britain, although it had originally been made for the American television market. Alf was thrilled to see his work interpreted for the big screen; another film followed in 1976. However, the following year was to be even more significant for it was then that agreement was reached for making the first series of television programmes by the BBC, and these were all filmed in Alf's beloved Yorkshire Dales. It was television that really rocketed James Herriot – and the actor Christopher Timothy – to full success. *All Creatures Great and Small* was regarded as compulsive viewing for millions of families; yet Alf Wight remained that same sincere, approachable man he had been in all those earlier years in the practice.

Alf Wight's achievements were recognised in the 1979 New Year's Honours List when he was awarded the OBE. He was given many accolades, including an Honorary Doctorate of Literature, a special British Tourist Authority Award – after all he created 'Herriot Country' – but a most important one was when he was made Life President of Sunderland Football Club. Still one more would give him great pride and joy – the new library at the Glasgow Veterinary School was to be called the 'James Herriot Library'!

Brian Sinclair died in 1988 – Alf felt the loss enormously, he was losing so many friends, and in 1991 Alf himself was diagnosed as having cancer.

Alf Wight's, or should I say James Herriot's, final book *Every Living Thing* was published in 1992. Donald Sinclair carried on working until he was 80, when a stroke brought his work to an end. James Alfred Wight lost his final battle in 1995. Donald Sinclair died a few months later.

No 23 Kirkgate, Thirsk is now the James Herriot Museum and the practice of Sinclair & Wight has moved to new premises on the outskirts of the town. Jim Wight has left his lifelong work, having served the community just as his father did before him. Other vets will carry the work forward, but they will never forget the example of Alf Wight, and perhaps they also will value their life's experiences as much as he.

The Society's first premises indicated by an X

The Skipton and District Permanent Benefit Building Society came into being on 1 May 1853, an inaugural meeting being held in the old Skipton Town Hall. Its first premises were in Providence Place, and were very modest.

It was George Kendall, a prominent Skipton businessman, who was instrumental in the formation of the Society, anticipating the advantages the district would derive from having such an organisation. He soon set out to find men who held similar views, and among them was Police Superintendent Beanland. They pledged him their enthusiastic support and personal assistance to move the idea forward to success. George Kendall and Mr Beanland both became directors, together with John Cragg,

Samuel Farey – one of the Society's founders

Joseph Thompson, Henry Swire, John Tasker, R Thornton, W Rimmington and R Crump. The first treasurer was Henry Smith. The first secretary was John Peacock, but it was his successor Samuel Farey who laid the firm foundation upon which the Society has been built. He was very interested in thrift and with providing opportunities for people of moderate means to acquire their own homes. Early patrons of the Society were men of influence in the town, such as Sir R C Tempest of Broughton Hall, J N Coulthurst of Gargrave House, Matthew Wilson of Eshton Hall, Rev W Cartman the headmaster of Skipton Grammar School and Rev P C Kidd, Vicar of Skipton.

In its centenary brochure it states that the Society's beginnings 'were modest, frugal,

The old Town Hall where the inaugural meeting of the Society was held on 1 May 1853

democratic and forthright'. Many of the older building societies were 'terminal' building societies, formed for the sole purpose of allowing a group of people to build, or buy, their own home and were wound up when the last person had done so. Skipton Building Society was not of that nature but was to be a 'permanent' building society.

In August 1853 the *Craven Herald*, three months after the inaugural meeting, printed in its leader:

The Society's first accounts

'This Society differs from the Old Building Societies, in this, that it is not established for the express purpose of building a certain street or row of houses, but what is much superior, it enables a man to build what he likes, where he likes, and as he likes; or, if a member prefers to buy a house, he can do so, and the Society, if they think the purchase a good one, will advance the money; and if he wishes neither to build, nor buy any buildings, he will receive $4^1/2$ per cent compound interest, calculated monthly, and can withdraw at any time on giving a month's notice; thus constituting an Investment good in itself, and especially suitable for the weekly savings of the working classes.'

A meeting was to be held that evening at the Town Hall when the first payment was to be made; 180 shares had already been taken up and it was expected that the number would reach 200. At the end of 12 months the Society had 190 members and had received into its coffers £2,325.

The directors watched with some apprehension, but interest and confidence grew as the number of accounts increased. It was not long before larger premises were taken at the Old Post Office on Ship Corner. Further expansion saw its headquarters moved to premises in Newmarket Street. There had been satisfaction for both investors and borrowers, and no doubt also for George Kendall – his vision was coming to fruition.

Arthur Smith became the Society's secretary in 1915; an outstanding man who altogether gave the cause over fifty years of his life. When he became secretary the Society had only 1,589 members, assets of £125,067 and a reserve fund of £2,868.

By 1922, when the assets of the Society had reached

The Society's Mortgage Department and Counter at the time of its centenary celebrations

£273,000, it was felt that in order to encourage further investments additional outlets should be opened. Through relationships which were developed with Messrs Ormerod & Ogden and Messrs J Entwistle & Co, agencies were opened in Nelson, Blackpool and Lytham. Gradually other agencies followed in many Yorkshire and Lancashire towns, and in 1929 the Society also began to operate in the London area.

In 1928, the Society's 75th anniversary year, its Head Office in Skipton High Street was opened by the Rt Hon Philip Snowden MP, a local personality and Chancellor of the Exchequer. The ceremony was performed with

a golden key which was presented to Mr Snowden by Mr J Hartley the architect, as a souvenir of the occasion. The following year the newly named Skipton Building Society had assets which exceeded £1,000,000, and from then on its progress has been steady and sound. By 1933 the assets had risen to £2,000,000.

Skipton Building Society 'took over the interests and engagements' of the Barnoldswick Building Society, where a branch office already existed in the town, in 1942. Harrogate was the first fully staffed, full-time branch when it opened in 1947. In 1953 the following branch offices existed: Barnoldswick – open every Wednesday and Friday; Earby – open every Friday; Cowling – open last Friday

in the month; and Harrogate – open daily. In addition to these there were 35 agencies, held in the offices of solicitors and other businesses, stretching as far south as Worthing, but no further north than Yorkshire or Lancashire. In earlier days agencies had been held in church halls and village schools!

During its centenary year Arthur Smith was able to report that the assets had risen to £11,714,090 (up £566,000 in 1952) and with a reserve fund of £590,555. After 75 years it still had only 7,576 accounts, now it had 27,016. No mean achievement for a society in a small market town.

It wasn't until 1962 that the first full branch in the South of England was established, at Guildford. In 1966 Skipton Building Society merged with the Ribblesdale Society, in 1974 with the Bury Building Society and most recently with the Otley Building Society. In 1974 Skipton Building Society's assets had risen to £100,000,000.

In 1991 the Society moved into new prestigious headquarters at the Bailey, near to Skipton Castle. However, it has already been necessary to extend these premises with an extension opened in April 2000. The Group's activities, now located in 80 branches, stretch from Aberdeen to Plymouth and employ approximately 3,000 staff – 1,200 of these based in Yorkshire.

Skipton Building Society has developed a group of subsidiary companies, offering a wide range of services. They include Connell Ltd, a 142 branch estate agency business, operating in 27 counties across the Midlands and South of England; and Eurodirect for customers wishing to pay their motor insurance premiums by credit.

The Society is still a mutual organisation and the seventh largest building society in the United Kingdom.

The earliest known references to brewing in Tadcaster go back to the 14th century, but our story starts in 1758 when David Backhouse, a local innkeeper, along with John Hartley the Postmaster, went into partnership and formed Backhouse & Hartley, brewers. At that time Tadcaster was enjoying great prosperity as a post and coaching town, with 50 stage coaches passing through each day. But as the railways steamed across the country and the industrial revolution developed, many coaching inns closed and Tadcaster ceased to be the main traffic route it had once been.

John Smith

However, the brewery remained and in 1847, 24 year old John Smith bought it from Jane, John Hartley's widow; it was the same year that the railway came to Tadcaster. By this time the enterprise was in a very run down state, but with the help of his brothers Samuel and William and sisters Elizabeth and Sarah the business prospered.

Foden Sentinel steam delivery wagon circa 1910

Original architect's drawing of the new brewery

Motorised dray circa 1920

Foden diesel wagon circa 1930

Traditional drinking habits were changing – the pint mug was giving way to glasses, and drinkers were moving to clearer beers. John Smith was determined to provide a quality beer with a popular taste and Tadcaster was the place to be, for it had excellent wells which were ideal for that purpose – the Roman name for the town was Calcaria, a direct reference to its magnesium limestone rocks, which give a hard water rich in sulphate of lime. John, who was a bachelor, was also a farmer and had interests in limestone quarries on the outskirts of the town; he was a familiar figure in Tadcaster as he rode around on his horse.

When he died in 1879 he left the brewery to Samuel and William as tenants for life, but as William was also a bachelor, the will stated that after their deaths the business would revert to Samuel's heirs. However, William bought out Samuel's share, and was joined in the business by Sarah's sons. Sarah had married H Wilkinson Riley but William, realising that the buildings would pass to Samuel's heirs on his death, and not to Sarah's sons, proceeded to build a new brewery on the present site and move the business to it. Samuel then established his own company, now Sam Smith's Brewery.

John didn't live to see the new brewery which cost £130,000 to build. In the early years the company's output was about 2,500 barrels a year, but by 1890 had risen to 15,000 barrels, then employing 100 people. When William Smith died in 1886 the business was left to Sarah's sons, Henry H Riley and Frank Riley, with the wish that they

adopted the surname Riley-Smith.

In 1892 John Smith's became a limited company with Henry Riley-Smith as its first chairman, a position he held until his death in 1911, when he was followed by his brother Frank, although he died in 1912. At that time John Smith's had over 250 horses pulling drays – some travelling as far as Pateley Bridge, on roads which often had many steep hills, both up and down. The railway also delivered much of the beer, with a 25 truck train taking beer to Sheffield on several days each week.

Between the years 1882 and 1939 the company acquired 20 local breweries, five maltings and several bottling stores in the North of England. At the end of the Second World War John Smith's established a market for Magnet Ales in Belgium, shipping casks from Hull to Antwerp, the beer being bottled in Belgium. In the 1950s when a dock strike brought deliveries to a halt, the firm arranged for two old Halifax bombers to be converted to carry seven-ton loads of wooden casks, which were rolled straight from the lorries into the bomb bays. Twice-daily flights from Sherburn airfield, near Tadcaster, ensured that the 'beer lift' got through!

During the post-war years the business continued to expand and Tadcaster became renowned as a brewing town. In 1953 John Smith's became a public company and towards the end of the decade, following many mergers and acquisitions, the John Smith Group was formed. By the 1970s 1,700 people were employed at the

Brewery; at the commencement of the decade John Smith's had become part of the Courage Group.

The current John Smith's company has been formed from the alliance of some of the greatest names in British brewing – John Smith's, Wm Youngers, T & R Theakston and Matthew Brown. Major expansion, thanks to a £23 million investment programme, has brought production to 2 million barrels a year.

Today John Smith's is part of Scottish & Newcastle plc, selling such international brands as Foster's, Beck's and Kronenbourg. A notice, which is still in existence at the Brewery, but which dates from the early years of the 20th century, tells us that the Darlington Licensees were announcing that no females were to be served drinks in pubs except from 12.30pm-1pm, and from 7.30pm-8pm daily – how things have changed!

Crosshills, 1906

G E Thornton
& Sons

I wonder how many family grocery businesses are still under control of the same family after almost 120 years, and also on the same site? – not many in Yorkshire I guess, if indeed any!

George Edward Thornton served his time as a joiner and cabinetmaker, later working as household joiner for Sir Isaac Holden at Holden Hall, at Oakworth, near Keighley.

His entry into the grocery business was as a manager (for three years) at the Co-operative Society Store at Shaw Top at Oxenhope. In 1880 George married Ann (known as Annie) Horner, whose family came from Maunby, near Thirsk, and the young couple made their first home in Oakworth.

However, in 1884 George, Annie and their first two children, Laura and Percy, moved to the present premises in Main Street, Crosshills, just a few miles from Keighley on the road leading towards Colne, and commenced business as a Grocer and Italian Warehouseman – it was their home and their work. Harold, their third child, was born there shortly afterwards. Later they moved to live at Lumley House

in Station Road, Crosshills, Lumley being Ann's grandmother's maiden name.

Soon George was able to show off his cabinetmaking skills as he fitted out his shop to meet the needs of the day. We must not forget that he would need a multitude of small drawers, each one holding some different loose produce – including such things as pepper, ginger, bicarbonate of soda, rice, sago, semolina, tapioca, caraway seeds, and porridge oats; none of these would be pre-packed in those days. Similarly there would need to be room for sacks holding flour or sugar, and on the counter would be large blocks of butter and cheese, unprotected from flies and dust, the heat of the day, or from the ash which dropped from George's cigarette end as he chain-smoked and measured out his customers' needs. Also there was a large tin of golden syrup – it was from this container that individual amounts were put into the jars or tins that customers brought for filling. The large tin was itself filled from a barrel of golden syrup which was lowered into the cellar from the street. One day someone did not turn the tap off properly on the barrel and the next morning the cellar floor was covered with about an inch layer of gloriously sticky syrup! Behind the shop Annie would make her delicious home-made cakes and fruit pies, each one tempting the local folk inside and each earning a few more coppers, helping to bring prosperity to the business and family.

In 1895 George opened a shop at Barnoldswick, just a few miles away on the Lancashire border – he paid his manager, Mr Ross, 27s 6d a week and commission of $1^3/_4$d in each £1; the boy who worked in the shop was paid 5s a week! When Percy and Harold became partners, and the business became G E Thornton & Sons, they nattered him to expand the business further and open other shops, but he became so fed up with this pressure that instead he closed the Barnoldswick shop during the period of 1914-18 war, when his sons were called up to serve their country, and ever since, the business has only traded from Main Street, Crosshills. George Thornton died in 1927 – his had been a full life, one which put much back into the local community, and particularly his beloved Wesleyan Methodist Church where he had served as a circuit steward and trustee, as well as using his fine tenor voice to good effect as part of the choir. He had been a quiet, friendly man with a genial temperament.

At one time the shop also acted as premises for a branch of the Bingley Building Society. Percy had always been more interested in accountancy than the grocery trade, although he kept the firm's books, and before the Second World War when the Building Society eventually moved to new

premises just around the corner, he managed it as well as working in the shop.

Harold Thornton married Ada Clough and they had one daughter, Joyce, who in 1945 married Sam Whitaker, who came from Oxenhope, and was a butcher. Members of the Whitaker family had been grocers and butchers in Oxenhope since 1764, but Sam's mother, Matilda Andrassy before her marriage, was a member of the family that is today renowned for marquees.

In 1948 Sam was offered Percy's share in the partnership, and he and Joyce came to live at Glusburn. That is how the grocery business in Crosshills came to sell cooked meats, which are still a speciality of the shop today. Harold, the last Thornton by name, died in 1968 at the age of 84, still working within the business to the last. Sam Whitaker has seen the company celebrate its centenary in 1984, and was still involved with the business at the age of 80.

Peter Andrassy Whitaker, the son of Sam and Matilda, was born in 1950 and joined the business when he left school in 1967. Today he, with the help of his wife Gillian and their children, continues to serve the local community as a family business always has – knowing many of its customers personally.

Sam Whitaker (centre) with Peter and his wife Gillian on the company's centenary, 1984

Chocolate Heaven Since 1911

Joseph William Thornton was a commercial traveller for the Don Confectionery Company in Sheffield. However, in 1911 he decided to open a sweet shop of his own – it wasn't to be just any sweet shop, but the best sweet shop in town!

The site he chose was right in the centre of Sheffield, at 159 Norfolk Street. But as money was short Joseph kept on as a traveller

and his eldest son, 14 year old Norman, became its manager.

About two years later Joseph took a second shop at 107 The Moor, Sheffield, but financial pressures meant that the family had to leave the leafy village of Hathersage and move to Sheffield to live over the shop on The Moor. The premises were not only a shop and their home, but also a small factory, for in the basement Joseph made a few simple hard boiled sweets such as fish mixtures and mint rock. Later they started making fondant-centred chocolates in the kitchen behind the shop.

Unfortunately in 1919 Joseph died. This meant that Norman had to take on the responsibility of running the two shops and also providing for his mother, two brothers and sister. In 1921 younger brother, Stanley, won a scholarship to Sheffield University. However, he decided it would be fairer to the family if he joined his brother in the business. By this time they had sweet shops, a fruit shop and the production areas in the cellar and

The very first shop in Norfolk Street, Sheffield, 1913

*The Archer Road factory in the mid-1930s (top)
and, more recently, production at the Castle Factory,
Belper, (above).
Right: Stanley Thornton beside an original Thornton
poster which he helped to design*

kitchen at The Moor shop.

With the business continuing to grow it was decided to form a limited company, J W Thornton Ltd. About 1924 Norman was told that unless he was prepared to buy the London Road property, which consisted of five shops and four houses, he would lose the lease. The price was £5,000 – he had to pay £250 down and make a capital return of £250 in March each year.

As a result of this financial pressure Easter became a critical season for the young company. Great efforts were made to boost Easter sales, including major sales advertising campaigns – outside the property they erected a large illuminated sign which was about twelve feet square. It could be seen all way down the Moor.

Another idea was to create spectacular window displays – one featured a large Easter egg in which live chickens ran about freely. Finally, they wrote people's names on the Easter eggs, adding the touch of putting each egg in a neat white box which prevented the lettering smearing. These initiatives caused a dramatic upturn in sales and as a result the mortgage was paid off.

Stanley took over the production of sweets, and studied food technology in the evening. About this time it was noticed that another retailer was having considerable success with slab toffee, and Norman suggested to Stanley that they could make a better one. As a result 'Special

The Sheffield Telegraph in December 1937 devotes a whole page to the Archer Road extension

Toffee' was born in 1925 and at one time accounted for over a third of the firm's sales. Even today, some seventy five years later, it is one of Thornton's most popular products.

One of the early shops was in Sheffield's London Road and among its rooms was one large one. They decided that this was the place to transfer the chocolate production which was then expanding.

Popular lines included rose and violet creams, fruit creams, and nuts and fruit dipped in chocolate, chocolate brazils being particularly successful.

Norman visited Holland and Belgium to see

how they made their quality chocolates. What he saw and learnt formed the basis for many of the improvements the company brought in over the next few years. Sales were now growing so significantly that in 1927 they decided to move production to a 'proper factory' – in fact a derelict building in Penistone Road, Sheffield. Prior to this the sweets had been delivered to their shops on a specially adapted wheelbarrow, but now they acquired a van!

on Saturdays! After the slump of the 1920s, more shops were opened in nearby towns and by the start of the Second World War they had about 35. The war proved to be a difficult time for Thorntons with several shops damaged by enemy action and sweet rationing that continued until the early fifties.

In 1947 a disused mill in Belper was purchased, the long rooms being ideal for enrobing chocolates. The 1950s once again saw a period of rapid expansion, not least as a result of their visiting Switzerland where they recruited a young specialist confectioner named Walter Willen. This was the birth of their Continental chocolates.

Stanley gradually took over the manufacturing departments and Norman concentrated on retailing, company development and finance. At seasonal times it was quite usual to work from 8 o'clock in the morning through to midnight, and even the shops were open until 9.30pm –10.30pm

Today manufacturing is centred at the purpose-built multimillion pound premises at Thornton Park, Somercotes (a few miles from the Belper factory) opened by the Queen in 1985. Thorntons PLC now has over 400 shops and over 100 franchised outlets throughout Britain and Ireland.

Wallace Arnold

Top: the first bus in the fleet in 1919 was this 28 seater
Above: a typical staff outing in the early 1920s

Robert Barr was born in Edinburgh in 1889, the first son of a Scottish farming family, but later he moved with his family to Woolley, near Wakefield. In 1904 he became an apprentice at the Bridge Garage and was paid 5s a week. It was a brave move for at that time no one really knew whether these temperamental and noisy vehicles would really succeed.

He bought his first motor vehicle, a Karrier, in 1912 — it was a dual purpose one: during the week he used it for carrying goods, but on a Friday night it quickly converted to an open charabanc to carry passengers to either the coast or countryside. Trips would include places such as Fountains Abbey, Rievaulx Abbey and Bolton Abbey — he saw them as memorials to a bygone age and delighted in pulling to the side of the road to describe the scenery to his passengers. This was the foundation on which he built his business, giving a clear public service.

In 1913 he bought a second vehicle and also took on Arthur Claxton, who had been in charge of him when he had been an apprentice. Arthur later became the company's chief engineer. During the First World War Robert continued with his haulage business but in 1919 he restarted his charabanc venture and added more vehicles to his fleet. In 1922 he took parties to Devon, Cornwall, Scotland and Wales. Three years later his fleet had grown to 30, and R Barr (Leeds) Ltd was formed.

Wallace Cunningham and Arnold Crowe had started a coaching business which they named 'Wallace Arnold Tours'. As early as 1922 they were advertising five day holiday coach tours to London or Edinburgh, and a nine day tour of the Scottish Highlands. In 1926, on the eve of the General Strike, they sold their business to Robert Barr for about £800. Arnold Crowe left the business but Wallace Cunningham stayed with the firm until his death in 1950.

From 1927 all new coaches had pneumatic tyres, which allowed the vehicles to travel at speeds of up to 20mph! It wasn't until 1928 that the last of the open charabancs was withdrawn and replaced by a fleet of fifteen purpose-built 'all weather' coaches. From those early days the haulage part of the business traded as R Barr (Leeds) Ltd and the coach business as Wallace Arnold Tours Ltd.

In the early 1930s Wallace Arnold offered a daily coach service from Leeds to Blackpool and in 1933 it organised its first continental tour, to the Black Forest and Berlin. In those days the coach had to be hoisted on and off the ship! In 1936 the company came to an arrangement with a coach operator in Cologne to provide the continental touring which saved transporting vehicles over the North Sea.

Throughout this period Wallace Arnold acquired a number of smaller businesses, and if the companies had a good reputation they retained the name. By the end of the decade the fleet had grown to 40 coaches. Coach travel, however, was still expensive and could only be afforded by the comparatively well-off. The company used quality vehicles, had couriers and travelling rugs, and stayed at the most exclusive hotels — it wasn't until after the Second World War that the market was opened to a wider public.

During the Second World War their vehicles travelled 20 million miles transporting soldiers to the front in France, and were even present at Dunkirk. At home they carried soldiers all over the United Kingdom. Robert Barr, one of the leading transport operators in Yorkshire, was appointed by the Minister of Transport as regional transport co-ordinator, a role he carried out while still continuing to manage his own business.

After the war, with the nationalisation of the haulage industry, his interests in that area were brought to an end; now he oversaw the expansion of his coach fleet. The first new, post-war Wallace Arnold coaches came into operation in 1946: one AEC Regal, a Bedford OB and two Leyland Tigers.

The bodies were by Duple, Scarborough-based Plaxton, and Wilks & Meade, an in-house coach building company acquired by Wallace Arnold in 1942 with a view to carrying out major upgrading of the fleet once the war was over. From now on all new coaches would be powered by the more economical diesel engines, and many pre-war petrol engined vehicles were later converted to diesel.

Among post-war company acquisitions were four small coach operators in Scarborough, and two in Paignton in Devon. These companies gave Wallace Arnold useful links in their development of coastal holidays, the two in Devon being very near to the Oswalds and Trecarn hotels in Torquay, which the company had purchased in 1945. The company at this time concentrated on the smaller 29 seater Bedford OBs, which were ideal for narrow roads, while the 33 seater Leylands, their larger coaches, carried out the longer journeys. Wallace Arnold had offices in ten northern towns and cities by 1948 and a total of 23 agents, as well as a London base in Croydon.

Early post-war publicity, including some brochures priced in dollars, was aimed at attracting American tourists to use their London base as a starting point, as well as offering the opportunity to travel by train to Leeds before embarking on a 'delightful selection of motor coach tours', including a 14 day tour of the Scottish Highlands costing $190 in 1949. The early 1950s saw the launch of the new underfloor-engined chassis; gone was the separate driver's

cab; now all new vehicles were full fronted and offered two passengers an uninterrupted view of the road ahead. New coaches could now be 30 feet long, giving the potential for 41 seats. Up to this time the livery had been summer ivory and carnation red; now it became all-over ivory. Their last half-cab coach was withdrawn in 1955. Continental tours were now expanded and eight tours were offered in the early '50s, ranging in price from 35 to 57 guineas, but in some cases only one departure was offered each year. The countries visited included Switzerland, France, Austria, Italy, Holland and Spain. In addition the company offered a number of day tours from Scarborough. By 1955 Wallace Arnold claimed to be carrying 25,000 tour passengers a year in its fleet of about 200 coaches. That same year it introduced low-priced off-season holidays for the elderly, one of the first operators to do so, thus opening up a potentially large market.

In the mid-1950s Robert Barr turned his attention to developing a chain of motor car dealerships, Wallace Arnold Sales & Service. Initially offering Sentinel lorries, and then Rootes Group cars, the company became the franchisee for the Nuffield Group which included Morris, Morris

Commercial, Wolseley and MG. A new 100,000 sq ft showroom was opened in Hunslet Road, Leeds, and the franchises for Vauxhall and Bedford were added. Now Wallace Arnold had a foot in both camps of leisure travel and would be well placed whichever way the future went.

The company also purchased Kippax & District, which enlarged its local bus operating business, and in 1959 this company, using six double-deck buses, carried 1.4 million passengers.

A new coach station and car park were opened in Leeds in 1957 and welcomed as a way of reducing congestion caused by coaches parking on city centre streets. Later in the decade Wallace Arnold ran daily express services from Leeds, Bradford and Huddersfield to Manchester's Ringway Airport and also to numerous seaside resorts. By 1959 express services were covering 300,000 miles a year and carrying 80,000 passengers.

By the 1960s the fleet of coaches was primarily

a mix of AEC and Leyland, but now coaches could be up to a length of 36 feet 1 inch, which generally gave a capacity of 49 seats, although smaller ones were more practicable for the narrow roads of Devon and Cornwall. In 1968 the company took delivery of its first 30 seat Leyland Leopard, Plaxton bodied, executive coach which displayed a new grey and white livery – this, along with a bold orange WA logo, became the new standard. From now on Plaxton were to be the company's main supplier of coach bodies, mainly fitted to Leyland chassis. By 1972 Wallace Arnold was offering 42,000 seats on its continental touring programme and coach/air tours from Manchester Gat-

wick and Luton. However, the end of the decade was to see a major drop in this market.

In 1980 the company launched Coach & Cruise – Wallace Arnold had linked up with P & O Cruises, using the liners *Oriana* and *Canberra* – with journeys to Nice, going outward by coach through France and returning by sea or vice versa. In-Tent was introduced by the group to provide camping holidays abroad for motoring families; it was sold on in 1984. These were the early days of a recognition of the dangers of smoking and in 1980 Wallace Arnold offered the first no-smoking tours. 1981 saw the introduction of its Pullman Express service from Leeds to London, using coaches equipped with toilets, video systems and hostess call buttons, but these were withdrawn in 1985, the same year that a new management team took over the running

of the company. From 1982 the company's reservation service has been fully computerised, with agents having full computer access from 1985.

In 1988 and 1989 Wallace Arnold was voted the Top Coach Holiday Operator. By now it was the second largest coach tour operator in Britain.

With the opening of the Channel Tunnel in 1994 new holidays were promoted using the Eurostar train service.

In 1997 the parent company sold its leisure division, which included Wallace Arnold Tours, to the management. The Wallace Arnold Group has gone from strength to strength and also operates seven hotels and a chain of travel agencies.

Since the successful management buy-out Wallace Arnold has continued to buy the best available coaches – Volvo chassis with Plaxton coach work – its purchases in 1999 and 2000 totalled 102, an investment of several million pounds, to bring the fleet up to almost 200 coaches.

Fittingly, in the last year of the second millennium, the company was again voted Top Coach Operator by UK travel agents.

Established 1876

H. Weatherhead and Sons (BUTCHERS) LTD

In some of our Yorkshire Dales family businesses stretch a long way back into history – H Weatherhead & Sons, butchers at Pateley Bridge, is one such firm. Whilst it may be a smallish business, tucked away in Nidderdale, its reputation for good meat and meat products is well known for many miles around. Customers frequently come from as far away as York for their pies, and perhaps not a little 'leg pull'! It is one of those shops where good service is often mixed with a little bit of friendly banter.

Ian Weatherhead's great grandfather, Henry Weatherhead, was a farmer at Bruce House Farm in Pateley Bridge. However he decided that he would become a butcher and so entered into an apprenticeship with John Atkinson at Ripley, near Harrogate, about ten miles from Pateley Bridge. The apprenticeship, begun on 1 January 1871, was to last for a term of five years. During that time he was paid £5 for the first year, increasing by £1 a year until the agreement was completed. The conditions of an apprenticeship in those days were very strict and forbade

Left: Founder Henry Weatherhead (nearest the camera) outside the first shop some time between 1900-1910.

Above: the same scene some years later with the Model T Ford van. The shop moved to premises just behind the van in 1927.

haunting taverns or playhouses, playing cards or dice or any other unlawful games; nor could he marry during the apprenticeship period.

When the period came to an end in 1876 he started his own business by selling meat on a market stall in Pateley Bridge High Street, outside the Black Bull Inn, which has since been demolished.

He slaughtered his animals at Bruce House Farm, but in 1881 he got permission to erect a new slaughterhouse at Book House Farm. In those days he had to provide a tooled, flagged floor, the walls had to be built of stone and be pointed before they were painted with lime; today the Government sanitation regulations are far more demanding than this.

Eventually Henry's sons, Harry and John, followed their father into the business, which created the name H Weatherhead & Sons. At this time, about the beginning of the 20th century, they took a permanent site at the bottom of the High

Henry Weatherhead and his wife, Annie

Street, where the Bridgeway shop is today. In those days the meat for the sausages was cut up by hand-operated mincers, and in the days before rusk was used as a binding agent, bread soaked in water served the same purpose – but it meant that sausages could only be kept for about one day. The first mechanical mincer that Weatherhead's had was powered from a belt linked to a paraffin engine.

Of course there were no fridges then – ice had to be brought from Starbeck, near Harrogate, and then placed in ice-filled cooling boxes. In the evenings the shop regularly stayed open until 10pm in order to try to sell all the meat, as it was very difficult to keep it fresh, particularly in summer. Deliveries of meat were made by horse and special butchers' carts – Harry's first commercial motor vehicle was a

model T Ford van. John Weatherhead eventually left the business to go and work in the Isle of Man.

Harry Weatherhead had six children – four girls and two boys. The boys, Joe and Edward (Ted), on leaving school around 1923 or 24, also joined the business. About this time Harry purchased the shop and house, as it then was, for £630. It was fitted out by a local tradesman, Allan Thorpe, and remains much the same today – except for some of the modern plastic fittings.

Harry's wife started the bakehouse. At first she only had a small gas oven which would bake just 12 pies at a time, but this was followed by a larger oven which was heated by a coke fire.

When the Second World War came Joe Weatherhead was called up to serve in the forces, which left only Harry and Ted to look after the farm and shop.

During the war years and up until 1954, meat was rationed, each person being allowed only a few ounces a week. When rationing finished the family was once again able to operate its own slaughterhouse, although by this time it had moved that part of the business to a site in

HOME-FED HAMS AND BACON.

Telephone 7.

H. Weatherhead and Sons,

Family Butchers.

High St., Pateley Bridge.

Established 1876

H. WEATHERHEAD & SONS

Picture taken 1905-1910 showing Mr Harry Weatherhead on the right who was Show President in 1957/8. On the left is Mr John Weatherhead and in the centre is Mr Lloyd Layfield. The Business is currently run by Ian and Brian Weatherhead and their wives.

Quarry Lane, where it is today.

In 1955 Ted's son, Ian Weatherhead, left school when he was 15 and started working full-time, being involved at the farm, slaughterhouse and shop – for many years he had been a true farmer's lad, but this was a proper beginning. Now they delivered meat and their other products on an open van, and this later developed into operating a number of mobile shops which visited houses and farms throughout Nidderdale five days a week.

As the years have passed, Joe Weatherhead has retired and Ian has been joined by his brother Brian, who was a qualified electrician but is now an expert baker and runs the manufacturing aspects of the business. Today Ian concentrates on buying stock for the farm and on the shop sales, readily exchanging banter with the customers. More recently, in 1982, Ian's son

Below: 1967 – Ian Weatherhead drives the company's first mobile shop.
Above: 1989 – Ian with brother Brian

Andrew has also joined the business.

H Weatherhead & Sons is one of those much talked of businesses which has been handed down from father to son, in this case on more than one occasion, something they are justly proud of, but they do not simply trade on their tradition. Today 30 per cent of their trade comes from outside the local area, people travelling from York and parts of Lancashire for their products, passing numerous other butchers on the way. Weatherhead's are still 'purveyors of meat', having their own livestock and land, still very much a quality family business – long may it continue to be so.

Yorkshire started to receive commercial television in November 1956, but another ten years was to pass before Yorkshire Television was conceived. It wasn't until 29 July 1968 that their new 'state-of-the-art' studios were completed. A wildly enthusiastic staff met to welcome HRH The Duchess of Kent (who was presented with a bouquet by eight year old Sarah, daughter of Donald Baverstock, the company's director of programmes) as she opened the Kirkstall Road Studios and put Yorkshire Television 'on-air'.

Our story begins in December 1966 when the Independent Television Authority announced that a radical change in the geography of ITV would allow the creation of a new franchise area – from 1968 a major networking company would be based in Yorkshire. The White Rose county was delighted, others less so – Sidney Bernstein, whose Granada company was already beaming into the area, is reported to have said, 'If the territory of Granada is interfered with in any way we shall go to the United Nations.' They had a franchise to cover the North West and Yorkshire – during the week, in our county, they were reaching 1.5 million people from their Emley Moor transmitter, and ABC took over at weekends; however, the potential regional audience was 6 million, and the national audience 25 million!

Lord Hill, the chairman of the Independent Television Authority, insisted that a new company should cover Yorkshire, one which was interested in Yorkshire and had its roots in the county. From the earliest days Leeds made a strong claim for the studios to be sited in the city, not least because there was a television studio there already.

On 28 February 1967 the region's newspapers

YORKSHIRE TELEVISION

carried an advertisement for the 'Appointment of Programme Contractor for the Yorkshire Area (Contract D) – All Week'. Among the early contenders for the contract was the Blackpool based Telefusion TV Rental group, headed by Sir Richard Graham – they were quick to point out that two of their directors lived in Yorkshire. Ten formal bids were received by the closing date – another had dropped out: that of Diddy TV, which was headed by Ken Dodd and included other show business personalities.

Although Telefusion Yorkshire Ltd was offered the seven day a week contract for the region, the ITA limited its total investment to £900,000 so that another Yorkshire bid – made up of the *Yorkshire Post* and Huddersfield, Halifax and Scarborough newspapers, Yorkshire Co-operative Societies, and some trade unions – could also participate by investing £850,000 with a further £75,000 being offered to Yorkshire universities. Telefusion also had to change its name and became Yorkshire Television Limited. The company obtained a five acre slum clearance site from Leeds Corporation on Kirkstall Road to build their proposed studios. Sir Richard Graham, a former High Sheriff of Yorkshire, became its first chairman, with G E Ward Thomas as managing director. Later Donald Baverstock was appointed its first director of programmes.

Work on the new studios began in July 1967. It was intended to spend about £4 million on the new centre, which would have three studios in Leeds, all designed to provide colour transmissions. There was the potential for a further two studios to be added later; other studios would be built in Sheffield, Hull and Lincoln. From the earliest days it was planned that the new station would provide about five hours a week of network programmes, and would concentrate on situation comedy, local current affairs and sport – 50 per cent of ITV's racing would be broadcast by YTV. In those early days the first executives and other employees were accommodated in the former Executex trouser factory, and raw recruits were rubbing shoulders with such television greats as Alan Whicker.

At the official opening important national figures such as the Prime Minister, Harold Wilson, the chairman of ITA, Lord Aylestone, and the Postmaster General, John Stonehouse were all present; also there were the Lord Mayor and Lady Mayoress of Leeds, Mr & Mrs John Rafferty, and the Lord Lieutenant of the West Riding, Lord Scarborough. After the Duchess of Kent had 'thrown the switch' to set the cameras rolling, the output switched to Headingley to cover the England v Australia Test Match. Cricket filled a large part of the day, but youngsters were not forgotten, for there was a preview of a puppet series *Jimmy Green and His Time Machine* and *Sugarball*, followed later by *Diane's Magic Book*, which featured 12 year old Diane Leslie Mewse, a pupil at Allerton High School, reading fairy stories, dressed in a Bo-Peep costume. At 6.35pm the first edition of *Calendar*

was broadcast, followed by *Mona McClusky*, a new film put out by the new company. At 7.30pm, not wishing to break with known success, it should have been *Coronation Street* but this was blacked out over the whole country by a technicians strike at Granada in Manchester, and therefore an old film was shown, followed by *World in Action*. Further material from YTV included a play, *Daddy, Kiss Me Better*, and a film made about Yorkshire and television, called *Made in Yorkshire*, which featured such famous Yorkshire people as Fred Trueman, Henry Moore, Michael Parkinson and Harold Wilson. After *News at 10* and the *Weather Forecast* cameras went live to a ball and cabaret being held at Leeds University to celebrate the station's birth. Close down was shortly after midnight.

To accompany a new network was the first edition of Yorkshire's own *TV Times*; it cost 8d, and had a picture of the Duchess of Kent on the cover.

Donald Baverstock was much respected as the man

The opening of YTV in July 1968 by the Duchess of Kent with YTV's first chairman Sir Richard Graham

behind the BBCs legendary *Tonight* programme – could he achieve the same success with *Calendar*? Unique in *Calendar*'s history the first programme was actually recorded at 5pm 'as live', one of those first presenters being a young Jonathan Aitken.

By the autumn of 1968 Yorkshire Television was getting into its stride, and was also starting to show good financial returns. Its programmes were receiving good acclaim, not only in their home county, but also from critics across the country, with such plays as *Funeral Games*, a black comedy, and *Inside George Webley*, a comedy series about a Yorkshireman and his wife. It wasn't long before producers, such as David C Rea, were exploiting the richness of Yorkshire's countryside in their films, and Alan Whicker soon discovered the rugged characters of Percy Shaw, the inventor of Catseyes, and Harvey Smith.

By the end of November 1968 the regional offices in Sheffield and Hull had come on line, and plans for the first Christmas shows were already finalised. Early in 1969 further successes came when it sold *Tom Grattan's War* to the Australian Broadcasting Commission, and, to CBS, an interview which Jonathan Aitken had had with television-shy Alice Longworth, the daughter of President Theodore Roosevelt.

The fourth studio was completed in the spring of 1969, in time to allow a full-scale recording of Handel's *Messiah*, which was then broadcast on Easter Sunday. However on 19 March a disaster beyond the belief of everyone took place – the 1,265 foot tubular steel Emley Moor mast collapsed. Could this be the end of television broadcasting in Yorkshire? Not likely. Although there was snow and icy conditions on the moors, VHF service was restored to 70 per cent of viewers within four days, and to almost everyone within four weeks. A temporary 680 foot mast brought in from Sweden was operating within 27 days, but in 1971 this was replaced with a 14,000 ton, 1,080 foot concrete structure.

By July 1969 the buildings were finished, the network was producing 14 hours of programmes a week, and its *Calendar* programme, with interviewers such as former Oxford don Austin Mitchell, was now known for its hard hitting attacks on subjects such as unemployment benefit fraud. Very different contributions were Yorkshire's *The Bruce Forsyth Show*, now widely used across the other networks, and *Sez Les* featuring Les Dawson. Still the true Yorkshire flavour came through as three nights a week William Foggitt, from Thirsk, gave his own weather forecasts, using signs gleaned from the 18th and 19th century.

Colour transmissions began on the 15th November 1969. Television would never be the same – colour offered so many opportunities, especially in the filming of wildlife and sports such as snooker. Another innovation at this time was the *Yorksport Sportsman of the Year Dinner*, where Billy Bremner, then captain of Leeds United, was voted Personality of the Year.

As the company entered a new decade it was announced that another transmitter would be built, to be sited at Bilsdale in North Yorkshire – it heralded the formation of Trident Television, a holding company which linked together Yorkshire Television and Tyne Tees Television. The agreement allowed both companies to retain their broadcasting identity. Figures released in May 1970 saw Yorkshire Television announce profits of £689,163 – 'a satisfactory figure' reported chairman Sir Richard Graham.

Three years after its opening, Yorkshire Television was praised by critics such as Michael Colbert, who congratulated it on its drama, documentaries, children's programmes such as *The Flaxton Boys* and *Follyfoot* (which received a special prize for the Best Children's Entertainment Programme from the Society of Film and Television Arts) and the semi-religious *Stars on Sunday* which attracted consistently large audiences. One of its documentaries *Out of the Shadow – Into the Sun* won the Golden Devil Award at the Festival of Alpine Films in Switzerland.

New viewer-friendly adult education programmes such as *Farmhouse Kitchen* resulted in the Kirkstall Road headquarters being deluged in 'fan' mail, each programme bringing in 15,000 letters.

When *Emmerdale Farm* was first transmitted it was planned to run twice-weekly – once again it would show the glorious Yorkshire Dales. Today it continues to run as *Emmerdale* – from autumn 2000 it runs five nights a week – to a very large audience. Many of these success stories in some way or other can be linked with Donald Baverstock who had been director of programmes up to 1973, but who then decided to become a freelance consultant. It was Barry Cockcroft who discovered and brought to our screens another truly Yorkshire character who would win the hearts of millions of people – Hannah Hauxwell. *Too Long a Winter* was to tell the story of her hard life in a remote dales village, just Hannah and her animals. Other programmes would continue to unfold her life's story.

Throughout its life *Calendar* has had to cover some gruelling moments, including the disaster at Lofthouse Colliery, the explosion at Flixborough, and the terrible scenes at Hillsborough. Within a very short time they were able to get Outside Broadcast units on these sites and provide coverage for the *ITN News*, as well as for the Yorkshire region.

Today glamour contests are often regarded as not being politically correct, but in 1974, and for the next 14 years, Yorkshire Television crowned their own Miss YTV.

In 1975, cool economic winds were blowing across commercial broadcasting and Trident Television was conscious of how it was being affected. However, by now the company was diversifying its interests into commercial radio and other leisure business, which even included 25 retail outlets in Australia where it sold and rented colour television sets.

Austin Mitchell had always been a popular face on *Calendar* but in 1977 he decided to stand as a candidate for the parliamentary seat of Grimsby, a seat he won by just over 500 votes, and therefore his contract with YTV automatically came to an end. He would be sadly missed, although of course he has appeared many times in his new role. However, there was still a strong *Calendar* team with people such as Richard Whiteley, Marilyn Webb, Geoff Druett and Alan Hardwick and as the

Calendar's first presenter Jonathan Aitken

'70s drew to a close YTV brought forward another innovative programme, *Good Morning Calendar*, Britain's first attempt at breakfast television.

The new franchise for Yorkshire ran from 1 January 1982, but would Trident Television be able to hold on to it? It seemed that some of the company's staff had their own ideas and that a consortium including some of them, called Television Yorkshire, might also make a bid. However, while the ITA gave YTV the broadcasting rights for Yorkshire, it decided that Trident Television should divest itself of its television business.

When Channel Four began transmission on 2 November 1982 the first person to appear was Richard Whiteley, as presenter of *Countdown* – a role he still has to the present day, having never missed a programme in all its long run.

In the Annual report for 1983 the chairman Paul Fox announced pre-tax profits of £4.97 million. That year they presented highly acclaimed series such as *God's Story*, *The Royal Family* and *Just Amazing*, which involved the motorcycle ace Barry Sheene.

In 1985 *Calendar* was awarded the Royal Television Society's Award for a Daily News Magazine Programme – sadly, that year its outside

Emmerdale's Alan Turner, played by Richard Thorpe, outside the 'Woolpack'

broadcast team was at Bradford City's Football Club when the horrendous fire broke out; it was praised for its sensitivity in such circumstances.

As the '80s drew to a close the company was floated and attracted potential subscribers. Whilst it celebrated 20 years on air it remained innovative, presenting a new 'soap documentary', *Jimmy's* – the story of St James's Hospital, and even won a contract to provide programmes for a satellite station.

Today Yorkshire Television is one of the largest ITV companies, producing over 1,000 hours of programming a year. It now employs about 900 people and serves a region of 6.5 million people. Its most modern studio, opened in 1997, covers 24,000 square feet, is the largest in Britain, and possibly in the world. Its award winning programmes – with over 300 national and international awards, including 5 International Emmy's (TV's equivalent of Oscars) – such as *Heartbeat*, *Emmerdale* and *Touch of Frost* are now enjoyed right across the world. *Calendar* continues to keep the region informed and entertained, just as those first presenters did way back in 1968.

Yorkshire Television is now part of Granada Media Group, although retaining its own broadcasting licence.